I0033626

Understanding the Financial Industry Through Linguistics

Understanding the Financial Industry Through Linguistics

How Applied Linguistics Can Prevent Financial Crisis

Richard Charles Robinson

BEP

BUSINESS EXPERT PRESS

Leader in applied, concise business books

Understanding the Financial Industry Through Linguistics:
How Applied Linguistics Can Prevent Financial Crisis

Copyright © Business Expert Press, LLC, 2021.

Cover design by Charlene Kronstedt

Interior design by Exeter Premedia Services Private Ltd., Chennai, India

All rights reserved. No part of this publication may be reproduced, stored in a retrieval system, or transmitted in any form or by any means—electronic, mechanical, photocopy, recording, or any other except for brief quotations, not to exceed 400 words, without the prior permission of the publisher.

First published in 2021 by
Business Expert Press, LLC
222 East 46th Street, New York, NY 10017
www.businessexpertpress.com

ISBN-13: 978-1-63742-058-4 (paperback)
ISBN-13: 978-1-63742-059-1 (e-book)

Business Expert Press Finance and Financial Management Collection

Collection ISSN: 2331-0049 (print)
Collection ISSN: 2331-0057 (electronic)

First edition: 2021

10 9 8 7 6 5 4 3 2 1

For my father, who has been my role model in how to understand and treat others in business and life. Rest in Peace, Dad.
And to my wonderful wife and my three sons, who inspire me daily.

Description

Imagine a collection of villages all beset upon by monsters. One village defeats their monsters using silver bullets. They convince all surrounding villages that their solution should be the **only standard**. The next village uses silver bullets to repel the monsters but fail! Why? Because the first village was fighting werewolves, the second village was fighting vampires.

This is our data challenge—recognizing not all problems are the same—and there are no single silver bullet solutions. There are many communities within financial services, each with nuanced needs that require slightly different solutions to address what may look like the same problem.

The financial services industry is unique for being based upon information and communication. It is the failure in understanding that multiple existing financial languages exist and pursuing interoperability that sits at the crux of financial crisis—not the lack of a single unified financial language. This book is an essential read for any professional dealing with data and information challenges.

The author presents a new, unique approach to broad industry issues, leveraging applied linguistics. They discuss how to break barriers that exist between language and data; the aim to make it easier for the financial industry (including regulators) to communicate—for the benefit of all investors.

Unconventional in the cross-disciplinary pairing of applied linguistics and financial services, it is practical and intuitive in pursuing solutions. While focused on financial services, the approach is relevant for other industries that have similar challenges.

Keywords

applied linguistics; data; standards; financial services; data management chief data officer; community of practice; silo; silo busting; interoperability

Contents

Foreword

Why did I write this book and who is it for? I mainly intended this for financial services professionals dealing with data and standards (from operations to front office to Chief Data Officers and other C-suites), policy makers in government (globally) who are using standards in their policies, and applied linguistics academics who may deal in the corporate world. As I worked with my editor, and began to expand on the points I was trying to make, I came to believe it does have a broader application. I hope those in other industries can utilize the principles here in applying solutions within their own communities. I also hope that if you are a student in either financial services or applied linguistics, that this text gives an accessible introduction to these areas.

That being said, regardless of levels of experience, from fairly new to the industry to seasoned, this hopefully will provide some new perspectives. I have found that even seasoned professionals tend to *stay in their lane* so to speak, and know one function or area of business deeply, without really knowing the others. So this would be informative for them as well.

Perhaps not-so-humbly, this is about a new approach to solving the data issues that plague firms in financial services, from regulators trying to regulate the markets and make sound policies, to data professionals trying to collect information from multiple sources and gain insights (and competitive advantage), to the everyday staff dealing with the same errors in communication occurring day in and day out. It is a broad overview of the securities industry, that deep dives in different sectors, all in the pursuit of illustrating how language and data seem to act as barriers, but it really is our approach that is the barrier. Instead of understanding and working with the data in the context it was created, we try to force the data to behave and act the way we want, to make it easier to fit within our individual world view.

This book will talk about the *financial industry*. That phrase in itself is immediately problematic—and ironically, one of the reasons for this book. *Financial industry* or *financial services* means many things to many different people. In a large set of cases, it refers to the retail banking, and even more so toward the credit card industry. It could be corporate financing. Or mid-market sector regional and local banking for the bulge bracket of small and mid-sized businesses.

To not belay, or belabor, the point—I will be focusing primarily on a segment that involves and interacts with what is typically referred to as *Wall Street*. But I wish to avoid the connotations even that bounding term implies (not that we will turn a shy eye toward the negative overtones and the propaganda-based politicking that involves *Wall Street* today and throughout history). Generally, I focus in the world of *institutional* business, centered mainly around trading of securities and financial instruments, with a touch about payments as they relate to institutional financial services.

I began in what we will refer to as *the financial industry* in the late 1980s, in back office and operational roles. (What you, or someone else may consider *the financial industry* may differ widely from my view— but we will clearly define that later—for the most part). Through the years, I have been involved in some of the larger transformative moments; Black Monday, expansion of global markets, dematerialization, the 1990s derivative crisis with Long Term Capital and Barings, transformation of partnerships to public firms, transformation of client server to the Internet, Y2K, September 11, Enron, repeal of Glass-Steagall, 2008 subprime and credit crisis, and resulting regulations like Dodd-Frank, Markets in Financial Instruments Directive (MiFID (I, II and III)), The Basel Committee on Banking Supervision (BCBS) 239, to name a few.

More so, I was involved in lesser known occurrences that, nonetheless, had impacts on my views of the industry; when Standard Chartered closed all its sub custody operations in Asia, watching phone calls and faxes slowly be replaced by proper messaging, founding of ISITC to work on best practices for messaging between firms, creation of the Financial Information eXchange Protocol (FIX) and the Financial products Markup Language (FpML), rise of *dark pools*, and revaluation of currencies like the Turkish Lira and Brazilian Real.

I was never a trader or investment banker, though operationally I worked next to them and had to jump through hoops to support some of the more esoteric things they tried to do. I tend to describe operations folks as the plumbers and electricians of the financial industry. Behind the scenes, making sure everything works, flowing from place to place. Operations tends to touch most aspects of the *industry*—as I will explain—with some specialties here and there. And mostly go unheralded or noticed—except if something breaks down or goes wrong. The thing is—something usually is going wrong, and operations people are frantically fixing it on the fly—the proverbial duck's feet under the smooth facade above. I have found this occurs for a vast array of reasons—but most herald back to differing perspectives and communities, context, misunderstandings, language, and—at the core—data.

My goal here is less about the mechanics, specific calculations, why specific investment decisions are made, and so forth. There are plenty of great books for that.[1] Instead, I try to provide some of my perspective—on why the financial services industry seems (and actually is) so complex, why efforts to *fix* perceived problems tend to cause more harm and not really solve for the actual problem, and how the diverse communities that exist will continue to resist *harmonization* and normalization. I hear "But that doesn't make sense. It shouldn't work that way." But there are reasons why—interdependencies, culture, context, and data all play a role. I do offer some practical advice, through anecdotes, case studies, and lessons learned. What I am offering is a path forward, a necessarily incomplete roadmap, but one that can provide ongoing guidance. I provide this, within a bound scope of how I am defining the financial industry, which

---

[1] While currently dated (as of this writing, the last editions were in 2007); *How the U.S. Securities Industry Works* (Hal McIntyre) and *After the Trade is Made* (David M. Weiss) give some good foundation to an operations view of the industry (though we do give a more generic, distilled overview we give in Chapter 1). For Derivatives, *Derivatives Demystified* (Chisolm—Wiley Finance) is a good primer.

does not encompass the entire financial industry (for reasons I will explain), but which I feel can be leveraged with some foresight and a grain of salt and applied to other industries and similar issues.

Finally, I will add a disclaimer here that these are my words (or others as referenced), and not the views of my employer or any of the organizations I otherwise belong to or represent.

Acknowledgments

I want to thank my editor, Jessica Moyer, who was able to sweep in and help organize my chaos. Without her, I doubt I would have gotten this past the first three chapters. She did much heavy lifting in driving research, structure, questions, and detail. We worked on this during the COVID-19 period where everyone was working from home, and she was saddled with teaching college classes remotely, which is no easy feat. Her contributions made this happen. Thanks to Christian Amport, KS brother and President/CEO of the Overshores Brewing Company in East Haven Connecticut, for helping visualize the map for Communities of Practice in Financial Services, and then drawing it for me. Go check his brew selection! Finally, a huge thanks to my cousin, Matthew Aldrich (BIGBADPIXEL Studios) for his rendition of the cover art.

Many deep thanks to Professor Scott Kiesling of the University of Pittsburgh, and Professor Tom Werner of Carnegie Mellon University, who both responded to a confused middle-aged financial operations guy trying to play amateur linguist (and obviously leveraging his alumni status at CMU and one of his son's attendance at Pitt in trying to ensure a response). They both graciously spent their own time to sit with me, over coffee and drinks, to discuss my premise and help validate my approach. Further, their continued support and guidance was invaluable.

To the organizations I belong to and have worked with over the years, and are mentioned in this book—the work individuals in these organizations do globally is critical, yet underappreciated, underfunded, and under supported. ISITC, FIX, SIFMA, APFF, ABAC, ISDA, OMG, X9, ISO, EDMC, Data Foundation, FINOS, and so on… I don't shy away from the criticisms I may have raised, but without these organizations, things just would not work at all. But we can and must do better.

To those I have had the distinct honor of working for and learning from; Bankers Trust (Jude, Theresa, Linda), Merrin (Emilio), Bank of NY (Kevin, Mr. Gennin), Omgeo (John, Tim), Barclays (David), Morgan Stanley (Ron, Jim, Ian, Mike), EMC (Alexis, John), Wipro (Ed, Beni),

Bloomberg (Pete, Steve, Dom)—thank you. I have taken something from each of you and learned so much on how to not just be a better professional, but a better person.

To those that I have worked and work with alongside—this book is for you. Hopefully it will make our jobs a bit easier. Jason, Gary, Marc, (all of the) Lisa's, Nigel, Corby, Karen, Tara, (all of the) Paul's, Tim, Jim, Tom (J&J), Genevy, Charles, Alex, John, George, Sherman, Mike, Francois, David, (all the other) Richard's, Kay, Pam... ok, I can't name everyone and I am horribly embarrassed I missed you if I did.

Thanks to my friends, who had to continuously listen to me yammer on and on about applied linguistics for the past three years and what I was writing. Brian, Lou, Paul, Keith, and Mark (and of course their better halves).

Thanks to the guys at Little Silver and Middletown soccer for being an outlet. And the ocean for the surf when I needed to clear my head.

My parents, Laura and Rich, who without, I would not be where I am today. From simple support to their constant encouragement and belief.

And to my family. Lisa, Dylan, Kyle, and Gavin. You are really the reason I do anything. Without your love and support, there wouldn't be any reward in anything I do. I thank you for enduring my (endless) lectures, unsolicited advice and professorial explanations and arguments. You continue to surprise me and make me proud with all you do.

CHAPTER 1

Introduction

A (Very) Brief History of Financial Services

While financial services would seem to have been around forever, modern banking systems were only established in the late 17th century, with international finance getting off the ground in the early 19th century. These new systems were based upon the practice of trade, lending, and commerce that had been around since before ancient Greece, typically linked to societies that had developed an agricultural base.

Historically, farmers and traders required funds in order to travel and carry their goods from field to market in different cities. Merchant lenders would give loans based on the grain and other commodities, and thus, enabled the expansion of such trade. Alternatively, loans would be comprised of seed, with repayment made from the profits of the resulting harvest.

Originally, trade occurred primarily on barter type systems (such as cattle and grain), with particular raw materials such as obsidian, becoming more central as trade expanded. As trade centers grew into population centers and cities, formal locations, typically based in temples or palaces, became centers for banking type commerce. Deposits could be made, and lending activities more centralized—as well as rules around the interest rates that could be charged. In Babylon, the Law of Hammurabi established formal laws, akin to similar rates and policies that had been developed in India under the Laws of Manu. Interestingly, both allowed charging of interest rates in the 20 to 30 percent range, according to clay tablets and other recording devices uncovered by archeologists.

Across different economies, rates would fluctuate in line with the prosperity (or not) of the society. In times of crisis, rates would rise, and would decline when times improved. One of the earliest debt crises occurred in Athens, resulting in reforms using the Laws of Solon.

Prior to these reforms, debtors would become slaves, and during the crisis, the economy began to spiral. One of the most significant acts was to forgive all the debt, free all the debt-slaves, and forbid the future use of one's person as collateral for loan.

During this time, empires began to establish taxes to fund their growth. As sophistication grew, coins came into play, firstly hewn as lumps from items with inherent value such as copper, obsidian, gold, and silver. Eventually, empires and merchant centers would formalize these into coins, with stamps of gods, emperors, or the merchant's seal for authenticity. This further enabled an economic system of lending, as coins could be hoarded and stored more permanently than grain or livestock, as well as relent to others. Systems of exchange would be created based on the knowledge of the stamped *minter* and the value was tied to it in relation to its intrinsic value, as compared to the intrinsic value of something from a different mint. Interestingly, the Inca empire appears to be the only one to never establish a monetary system; all needs were met by the ruling system, based on the exchange of services in a communal work system known as mink'a.

Through Roman times, various empires would revise and evolve rules. In China, early banknotes would be created using leather squares, and later was home to the first known use of paper currency. Jewish, Christian, and Islam religions, all released interpretations condemning and prohibiting the use of interest, and soon after came ways of going around those prohibitions. Banking in the western world mainly ceased after the fall of Rome and the subsequent rise of religions and their restrictions. The exception was among Jews who were allowed to charge interest on loans to those not of the Jewish faith. Christians would take out those loans, and by paying interest, not charging it, the rules of both faiths were satisfied.

By the 11th century, legal fictions and other means were in common use to get around the ban against usury. The advent of the Crusades, and the need to fund these expensive campaigns was a major cause for the re-emergence of banking. Monarchs looked to tax trade to raise money for the Crusades and other empire building efforts, while religions looked to impose rules to control trade. Merchant banks in Italy, exemplified by the Medici Bank, began to flourish. These early *merchant banks* began nearly where the original seed lenders began—enabling funding of crops and trade. Banking systems formalized lending systems for borrowing money, to finance long trade journeys, or provide financing to merchants and farmers. Insurance also came into play, helping farmers or merchants in cases of crop failure.

Governments and other organizations continued to create new products and services for customers, with the goal of creating investment in projects and businesses as the driver of their business models. Enabling banking within their countries or empires enabled trade with other countries and empires, and thus expanding their economies. As these systems matured, and expanded with colonialism, they also dealt with emerging regulation.

Investments were created to fund exploration and expansion in colonies and the New World. Companies were formed with the concept of private stock given to investors. These companies had a single purposes of discovery or trade, and upon completion of the mission, they would be dissolved and the money paid back to the investors—the stock holders. All the while, the data captured was mostly the recording of general accounting information. The data was confined and limited to the investor group, any banks or governments involved, and those executing the mission. Double sided accounting was in full use, and the ledgers were the central storage of record. Paper certificates, like bank notes, were given to investors or lenders as their record. Indeed, modern banking deposit systems evolved out of the Italian systems, which were developed to help avoid the frequent handling of cash. These private company arrangements simply took this concept one step further. The creation of the Dutch East India Company and the British East India Company caused this model to change again. Not only were stocks offered to anyone (as opposed to only a private few), via the newly created Amsterdam Stock Exchange, but the company was envisioned to continue to *live on*. Instead of just one ship and voyage, the company would fund multiple ships and voyages. This raised the likelihood of success, as well as creating profit for everyone, which could then be used to fund future ships and voyages.

This was not the whole of banking, as all the previous activities continued. Governments, emperors, and monarchs, all required money to wage wars and encourage trade, as well as to continue to live in style. (Spain would overborrow while trying to defend its dominance of the seas and colonies in the 16th to beginning of 17th century, the country would actually become bankrupt four times under Philip II and III up through 1607, and another five times under future rulers through 1666). Local merchants still required loans for expansion, or to cover materials and expenses. Governments continued to enact laws that limited certain practices that, much like the Laws of Hammurabi, Manu, and Solon, created rules on chartering, rates, and lending. Throughout this time, goldsmiths would store wealthy merchants' gold, and then in turn would lend money by issuing paper certificates. These would eventually become banknotes. A number of other advances occurred, from publications like Adam Smith's "An Inquiry in the Nature and Causes of the Wealth of Nations" in 1776, to the establishment of Central Banks such as the Bank of England. These were a means of managing monetary policy, interest rates, and overall money supply for a formal state or nation and were typically chartered by the government as a monopoly.

The variety of investments available, and types of trade, accelerated in the 20th century, leading to a proliferation of data being created for many different purposes. Until the mid to late 1900s, the main levers of economies focused around debt, currency strength, reserves, and the type of financial products easily relatable to the early days of ancient seed and livestock lenders. However, the 1960s saw the creation of new types of financial products not directly related to any actual activity—the repackaged loan that was offered to a new *secondary marketplace*. Essentially, a bank would make a loan, but it would not itself then hold on to the loan. It would repackage and *sell* the loan to an investor.[1] Still, there were no insights around the differences between very similar products and different kinds of loans.

During this time, banking and the financial systems were viewed mainly from an accounting, macroeconomic, and microeconomic viewpoint. In that way, any data recorded and collected was (and in many ways continues to be) in that vein, for those uses. The advent of

---

[1] Typically said to have originated at Bankers Trust Company under Charlie Sanford.

computing enabled some data capture, but until storage and processing power limitations were made more trivial (arguably somewhere between mid 1990s and early 2000s), data was not particularly accessible. The recording of data was focused on accurate books and ledgers, as opposed to the trends. This changed in the 1990s, with the greater computer power and storage. This allowed for the growth of analytics, from a programming point of view and created an explosion of data as the Internet Age came to life. The introduction of *alternative* and nontraditional financial data into decision making shifted financial data from something to be simply recorded to more of an asset in and of itself.

To most people today (circa 2020), the rhetoric of *Wall Street* versus *Main Street* encompasses the entirety of what is considered to be the financial services industry. Movies, from the seminal *Wall Street* to *Boiler Room* and *The Big Short*—while accurate—have shaped perceptions into ones that ignore most of the *hidden iceberg* that actually exists. Additionally, while there may be a recognition of the complexity of the business, there is still a misperception that it could easily be made simpler and easier to understand and control through some basic changes. While I agree there are things to be done, and need to be done, I am trying to avoid direct answers and instead wish to provide a better foundation of understanding so that such decisions can be better informed—for policymakers, industry members, as well as the layman.

Here Comes Data (and Standards)

Until relatively recently, the focus on data (which I include *information* as part of) was purely a store-and-retrieve function. Relational databases came into use as a response to needing to organize rapidly growing (in size and variety) and changing data. Data was captured as it was, and depending on where it came from, often without much thought to its need or use outside the immediate function in which it resided.

In trying to deal with this complexity in process and data, there is a natural resulting drive toward creating and utilizing standards to enforce some sense or baseline for common understanding. In manufacturing, the Industrial Revolution was fueled by standards in interchangeable parts. Disciplines like engineering demanded clear standards for tools and machinery to work properly. In the information age, data is viewed as the nuts and bolts, the interchangeable parts, required to drive the information economy. It would make sense, then, to explore standardization of data, and the systems and processes that use data.

With the increased scrutiny of data from every perspective, whether the media, regulators, or clients, the ability to get a handle on the information and drive standards that can be embraced by all has become both increasingly important and difficult. As we try to bring the *same* data from multiple, different sources together to get a single, unified view, it has begun to be a question if that similar seeming data really is *the same*. The advent of modern data management (and the *Chief Data Officer*) brought new scrutiny on data, and by association, standards. Suddenly, new questions were being asked. How do we create data, understand its context and lineage, and ultimate meaning? How do we share data and communicate effectively, yet ensure we have common understanding and agreement? Many point to standards to solve a bulk of these problems, but this simply shifts the problem. Who is creating the standards? Does the resulting standard reflect the understanding of the group it was intended for? Can it work for a group it was not intended for? Doesn't the virtue of something being a *standard* mean that it should apply to everyone, regardless of what they are doing?

Further, there is a standing debate on the impact of standardization on innovation and flexibility. I hope to help inform this discussion. There is a nuance that tends to be forgotten, or not understood, when this debate is had at an aggregate level. Again, our hidden iceberg shows itself here. There are multiple standards organizations that may or may not work well together, and have varying level of prestige and power among policy makers that may differ from user perceptions.

Standards work tends to be an esoteric exercise that is somewhat opaque to the everyday user. However, it influences data, perception, and interpretation in ways that may not have been intended. There are often disconnects between the standards community and the communities their work influences—usually not through any fault or intention—but that aspect cannot be ignored. These disconnects have an impact on essential data that is relied upon by the industry and those that regulate or follow it.

Data pulled from one source typically carries some inherent bias, inferred meaning, or other context that makes it different from seemingly *like* data from a different source. Data are like words in a language. And like words in a language, without the included context of its source, its *community*, words (i.e., data and standards) can be misinterpreted. This has an impact on standards—both in the creation of standards, as well as their use and implementation.

For example, the word *jumper* in Queen's English means *sweater*, which is a far cry from American English, where (depending on region) the same word will usually be interpreted as a person physically jumping or the cords needed for charging a dead car battery. Different communities—even if they have a common base for their language—will continuously evolve and diverge from each other in use and meaning. In the same way, data and how it is defined will evolve and diverge in different communities, even if they interact with each other.

Over the past 50 years, technology has rapidly evolved and changed. Approaches on how to store and classify even the simplest data point, such as a date, have multiple standard methods. Changes and differences vary due to influences as diverse as technology or culture, but continue to evolve. This is due to new abilities and understanding in technology and data, as well as how globalization and culture change how certain data is viewed.

The tech craze and the *hot tools* of the month continue to confuse the average business professional in finding the best way to focus on their data. In *The History of Databases*, it is said "The history of databases is a tale of experts at different times attempting to make sense of complexity."[2] We have gone from punch cards and flat file data storage, to hierarchical and network modeled database management systems (DMBS), to the relational database. How we structured and stored data is what drove us how to define it—and we are now in another revolution as relational databases are rejected and redefined with the advent of NoSQL and NewSQL. Yet, all of this tends to come from the technical disciplines.

---

[2] Avant.org. 2014. "A Brief History of Databases." *Avant.org/Project/A Brief History of Databases.* http://avant.org/project/history-of-databases/ (accessed January 4, 2021).

Data practitioners are familiar with words like ontologies and semantics, but many do not appreciate that these concepts have existed for decades (and sometimes centuries!) within the discipline of linguistics. Further, technologists generally do not have formal native training in linguistics and can tend to believe that their code is able to normalize all meaning. This can be particularly dangerous.

What to Expect in This Book

This is where the critical pivot point of my forthcoming discussion takes place, and where I believe I am bringing a new perspective that could improve multiple aspects of the financial industry—ranging across operations, data management, communication and interoperability, policy making and regulation, and transparency and accessibility. I introduce applied linguistics, and discuss how incorporating some of the methodologies and concepts of this discipline (primarily from the socio-linguistic standpoint) can accomplish this improvement.

So, then, the goals for this book are practical, yet bold. First, we hope to provide a foundation based on three pillars:

1. A functional view of the financial industry (with a bias toward the operational flows of the securities business)
2. An understanding of the various standards and tools in use (and why)
3. An introduction to applied linguistics and its importance in evaluating and making decisions based in the other two pillars

Based on this foundation, I will present a model for viewing the world of financial services, through the lens of applied linguistics. Through this lens, we should better understand the various communities and vested interests across the industry and how they interact with each other (and perhaps a little bit on why they behave the way they do). This, in turn, should inform how we view, create, apply, and implement standards and best practices. This has a broad impact globally across policy makers and governments, as well as organizations and individual practitioners. It should act as a call for better coordination across differing standards bodies, as well as a multitude of industry organizations. Finally, understanding the role and nature of language, the communities that exist (and those that are yet to be created), and how these evolve and change, is a critical capstone to ensuring we continue to address the practical and achievable while striving for the theoretical and visionary goals of all interested parties.

Data that has been isolated on islands presents a more difficult problem, as it has no use if it cannot be defined and understood. An analogy would be islanders isolated from the world that have created their own language over the generations, and have had no contact with anyone. Their language, customs, likely everything they do would not be able to be understood by someone suddenly discovering them. It would take enormous effort to translate the language and understand the culture fully, with the complication of the act of interacting with them would itself change their language and culture during the process.

More Clarity on the Problem

Now, imagine some accounting system that just takes in inputs all day, all year, for decades, and just runs and runs. But it actually doesn't send anything back out… it just keeps taking inputs, and doing its calculations. Maybe it creates a report that someone takes, who then uses a couple of numbers from it to enter into some other process. But, generally, it's just there. After 10 or 20 years, someone decides to find out what this computer system is doing. But over the years, accounting standards, accounting terminology, even *computer* languages, terminology, and how we labeled columns and tables have changed so much in that period, that this is essentially a new or rediscovered language, especially if the creator has left the company. Now after three new people, the people left were just trained to take the report, look at this space on the page and use that number as an input, without knowing the meaning or how it was determined.

Our current state has made it virtually impossible for us to look at data *in the wild* and connect it to the appropriate context or use. Data exists all over the place. It is stored all over by specific people for specific purposes. Since *they* knew the specific purpose, they didn't necessarily indicate the purpose of the data. So, now that data gets packaged in some report, or even the full database is sent out, or someone from some division gets access to look at it. Essentially now, that data is *in the wild*, without context.

Now, assume it's not just the original data that got stored, but also data that was created based on that data, and even data from elsewhere (meaning that original data isn't present, and you don't even know that it was used). Someone can guess what it all means, or is supposed to mean, but without going back to the original builder/users/community (or remaining caretaker), it's likely they will interpret it wrong, or from their own perspective (which, well, would also be wrong). And if it's just a caretaker, you likely will start to fall into the island problem as well, which was illustrated earlier.

People assume that when they come across a piece of data that is labeled a certain way, like "Name", they automatically know—and assume—what it means. Unless you know the cultural differences in China (and other Asian countries) that last names come first, you will incorrectly assume someone's first name is their last name. If you come across a date labeled "Year" and it says "19", you will assume 2019 (and usually would be right), unless it's an old data set about past projections and the date is actually 1919.

The way we store data is biased, but our bias isn't visible when that data is *in the wild*, so it becomes disconnected from the appropriate context and use. Most will not realize this and use it for their own purposes and in large samples. The errors may work themselves out, and the anomalies get smoothed over—or it could simply create a completely false result because the foundation is based on faulty premises.

A Word on Expertise

In all these cases of data—it is created by experts. This label of Subject Matter Expert (SME) gets thrown around, and when looking at information, it is wise to find an expert to help interpret it. However, many may present themselves as experts, but don't have hands-on knowledge, or have limited exposure to the actual subject matter. There have always been arguments over *book* education versus hands-on experience in building expertise, which many times comes down to theoretical versus practical experience. However, self-awareness is difficult, and has gotten worse in the age of Google where many people believe they can be as educated as a doctor by reading WebMD. Additionally, experts in adjacent areas may try to infer how one thing works based on their own frame of reference. But being a subject matter expert in one area does not make anyone a subject matter expert in any other subject, regardless of how closely they may seem to be related. In other words, you would not trust a pediatrician to treat your cancer diagnosis.

I started out in Global Custody in the late 1980s and early 1990s. I dealt with settlements across the globe, including Euroclear and Clearstream (back when the *Bridge* existed[3]), physical settlements in Thailand (I will tell you later about the bike messengers and settlement confirmation by telephone), the creation of CREST, and change of settlement in the UK.

However, a walk across the room to the DTC settlement people (*domestic settlement* for U.S. based people), seemed like a world away. Even after three years of settling securities globally including through our U.S. based *domestic* settlement people, I was never an SME in the U.S. domestic settlement, until years later when I spent stints in those roles, discovering some differences that could be described as nuances, and others that were fundamentally distinct and unique.

As an SME with experience in both areas, I can categorically state that Global and U.S. Domestic settlements are two completely different areas of expertise. No, it does not make sense that this would be true. But it is. To be honest, most of what I encounter can be described that way. When I try to explain something to a nonexpert, they typically react in disbelief. "That's impossible. Nothing would work that way. It doesn't make sense." We might even go as far to say that if your SME doesn't immediately follow a solid statement with "…well, most of the time, that is" or a "…but…" or "..except when…", then there is a chance that they are not an expert on that specific subject.

I could try to simplify, and tie everything up in a nice little bow. But, to tackle the really hard problems, I believe that you need to know the golem in the gears (so to speak). Decisions that ignore the nuances can have ramifications.

---

[3] You can Google that.

The other pitfall of expertise is bias. There is always a bias toward a specialty, a philosophy or way of thinking, selection bias in the people you speak to or subjects you follow, and finally, an undercurrent of confirmation bias that shields you from seeing a different perspective. There is an excellent book I recommend, "The Death of Expertise" by Tom Nichols, that gets further into this topic and how there is a trend to believing "all voices, even the most ridiculous, demand to be taken with equal seriousness, and any claim to the contrary is dismissed as undemocratic elitism."[4]

---

[4] Nichols, T.M. 2017. *The Death of Expertise*. New York, NY: Oxford University Press.

CHAPTER 2

Defining *Financial Services*: Roles and Interactions

To provide a basis to work from, I would like to walk the reader through some basic *high level* roles that are used in regular discussions about the industry. This will form the basis of what is *In Scope* in regards to the processes and players to which this book discusses and refers.

More importantly, I will express what is out of scope, and why, as I need to bound our discussion. The financial services world is vastly complex and interconnected. For example, in discussing payments in regards to security investments, I can easily follow the connections into corporate treasury desks. This would expand into the roles they play at firms from McDonalds to IBM to Subaru to Sony, how they manage their funds and balances across the world, how it impacts the financial system (macro and microeconomics), and firms acting on their behalf (process and operations).

This, while important, can be built on with this book as a basis, as opposed to trying to cover every possible topic between these covers. Further, there are subjects where I have insight, but not core expertise, such as retail, credit cards, payment processing, and more. Best I stick to what I do know, and that in which I am a subject matter expert, which is quite enough to fill the pages here and still not give this topic full justice. Even more important, differences in language and processes skew them just outside our core expertise. This point you should understand and agree with at the end, if I have done the job.

Much of the content in this chapter has been adapted from the training I have done over the past 20 years, mostly informally. It began as an introductory training to help new programmers who didn't have exposure to any formal experience in financial services or operations. As new audiences were added, versions of the training have been given to individuals with varying levels of experiences, regulators, and at trade shows.

When a Trade Is Not a Trade

There is a common offhand saying in our industry; "a trade is a trade is a trade." At its core, the financial industry is a deceptively simple thing—it is one party or entity that exchanges some kind of asset with another party or entity.[1] Of course, I already have begun to hedge, and qualify my words with *party* or *entity* and *some kind of asset*. Because these are not precisely correct, all the time. But I will come back to that later.

I will start with some very basic concepts. Note that I will continue to evolve these definitions as we continue. As you will start to see, there is always an opportunity to say "Well, not *really*" for any given description, based on a certain context. To keep things simple, I will work with the constructs of the equity market. I will dive into other asset classes later, and illustrate what is different across contexts of asset class, functional roles, and other type of communities, but for now, it is important to put down a basic foundation on which to build.

Settlements—Exchanging Assets in the 1990s.

It was 2 a.m. and I was sitting at my desk on the 2nd floor of Harborside in Jersey City. Working the midnight to 9 a.m. settlement operations shift, ISO 7775 messages were coming in, indicating trades that were being settled by the Thailand subcustodian. But it was nearing the end of the day, and a few higher value trades hadn't yet settled. So, I dialed up the local contact number with the list of trades still pending for that afternoon.

Soon I learned, the delivery for $10MM shares had failed because when they tried to deliver, the person they talked to said they didn't know anything about it. Quick call to the client, to call the counterparty, confirm they have instructions in place, and a call back to the sub custodian.

---

[1] Some in depth reference texts are: Harris, L. 2002. "Trading and Exchanges: Market Microstructure for Practitioners" Oxford University Press; and Maginn, J.L., D.L. Tuttle, J.W. McLeavey, and J.E. Pinto. 2010. "Managing Investment Portfolios: A Dynamic Process" CFA Institute Investment Series Book 32, 3rd ed. John Wiley and Sons.

"OK, he's just left on his bike with the securities. He's supposed to call in the next 20 minutes, but traffic has been heavy today."

Yes, bike messenger, riding through Bangkok, with our client's $10MM worth of share certificates. And a $10MM settlement at risk because of heavy foot traffic in the city, and the person working the desk at the counterparty didn't know to just accept the delivery.

The Traders and *Wall Street*

There are many books that provide an excellent history of Wall Street and modern finance, which I lightly covered in the introduction. I don't assume you know any of this, but in this book, I want to focus more on the processes and relationships versus in depth history or simple mechanics. Recalling our *brief history*, up through the late 1700s, brokers and dealers would meet along the physical Dutch Wall on Wall Street to obtain funding for various mercantile needs, in a basic copy of traditional Dutch exchanges. This became formalized in 1792 when 24 brokers signed an agreement to establish and restrict membership and standardize rules for a public stock exchange.

In the ensuing 200 years, growth and maturity of the markets necessitated new processes and players, but at its core, there are still only a few basic roles that exist in exchange-based activity.[2]

- Broker/Dealer: A person or firm that buys and sells securities for their own account, or on behalf of a client. While many times used interchangeably, a *broker* trades on behalf of someone while a *dealer* trades for their own account.
- Exchange: A marketplace where buyers and sellers of assets meet to trade, such as the Amsterdam Stock Exchange.
- Central Counterparty: An entity that inserts itself in-between buyers and sellers for trades. This is done to reduce risk (I will explain later).

---

[2] OK, so someone will say, "but investment managers and the buy side can access exchanges and dark pools!" Which is true, and we will get to, but outside the *basic* operation of an exchange.

- Depository: An entity or other facility where records and/
  or physical assets being traded are held for safekeeping and
  record keeping purposes.

Remembering that the end goal is less about the mechanics, and more about the relationships and interactions, I want to focus more on the purposes and goals versus nuts and bolts. At a very basic level, a Broker/Dealer wishes to buy something. Figure 2.1 illustrates a simple basic interaction and flow for a broker to broker transaction (with more explanation in Table A.2 in the Appendix). They will typically go to an exchange to find some other broker/dealer who is looking to sell that same something. The exchange, as a concept, could reasonably be anything from a list of phone numbers for other brokers/dealers, to an instant messaging system like Instant Bloomberg ("IB") on Bloomberg, to a formal exchange like the New York Stock Exchange.

Individuals doing this part of the role are the *traders*. Traders will record each trade they do, and who they did that trade with. For example, let's

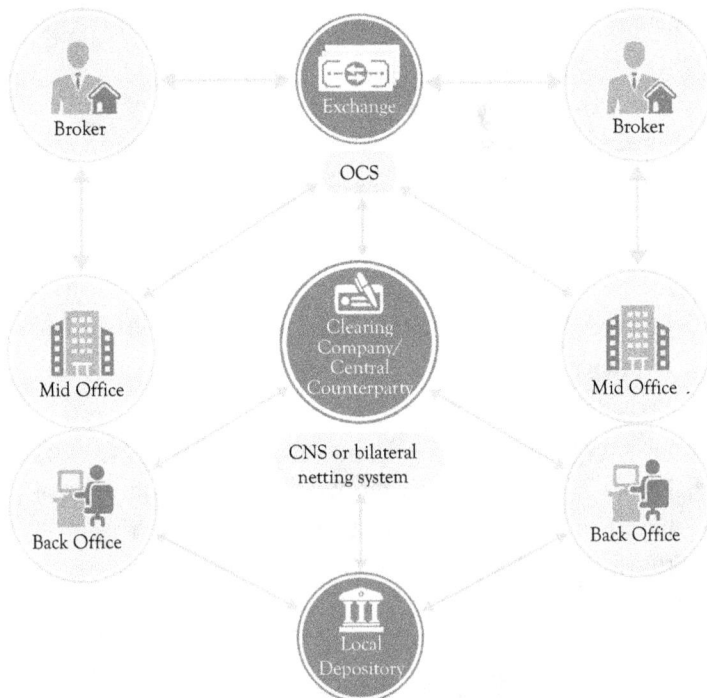

Figure 2.1 Basic view of a local brokerage flow

assume broker/dealer A bought 100 shares of IBM common stock from broker/dealer B for $150 (United States Dollars) on the New York Stock Exchange. When shares are bought or sold, the actual exchange of asset for cash does not happen right away. There are many reasons for this, which I will get into in a later chapter. Traders, executing many trades a day, with many different counterparties, need to make sure at some point that they recorded their information correctly, and ensure that their counterparty did, as well.

At some point after the trade is done, the two parties to the trade contact each other to verify they got the details correct. This can be done in many different ways—from a phone call, to fax (think pre-1995 e-mail), to formal systems that many exchanges run, called *Order Comparison Systems* (OCS). In an OCS, each side inputs what it recorded as the agreed details of the trade. That gets matched to each other and to the records of the exchange. If there are any disagreements, everyone will be notified to research and fix the error.

Finalizing and Settlement

As long as all trade details are in agreement, the process will move to settlement. Prior to the late 1990s, many—if not all—settlements could be in *physical* form, depending on the country and type of asset. Messengers would carry satchels with physical certificates to the offices, and then the receiver would call their bank to release the payment to the seller.

Where there are many firms trading, many markets have instituted a safeguard called the Central Counterparty (CCP). In the U.S. market, the main entity is the National Securities Clearing Corporation (NSCC). At a high level, all participating firms put up *guarantee money* to fund the NSCC. In return, the NSCC will insert itself between every transaction due to settle, and will guarantee every transaction will settle. This effectively reduces overall risk in the market. The number of trades that need to actually settle is vastly reduced. This means that shares, and money, does not need to be *locked up* in order to satisfy every transaction. Instead, only the effective net amount of shares and money is required. When spread across all activity, the cash component is further optimized, meaning that cash can be used for other activities.

The final part of settlement is to ensure every party has the cash and/or assets they owe in their holdings. Most markets have instituted a *depository* for this function. The depository acts like a bank for trading firms, where physical certificates could be *deposited* and held in a vault. Most markets today are *dematerialized* and the depository is responsible for keeping electronic record of what each participant has in their accounts—and to make the appropriate accounting entries when appropriate. For broker activities on the exchange, the CNS (Continuous Net Settlement) system will typically inform the brokers what movements will be made in their accounts. Each party to the trade is making entries to record trade information in their internal systems and records throughout this process; so at this point, there should be no surprises.

Operationally, each of these steps could feasibly be handled by a different firm. An *Executing Broker/Dealer* would be a firm that has a membership and rights to use the exchange facility. The *Clearing broker* would provide services to ensure settlement, and acts as the record keeper for the executing party. They may actually contract out to a local settlement agent, as there are typically specific rules on who may belong to a depository or CCP and use those services. At this point, let us note that there could be nine different firms, computer systems, and individuals involved in a single simple trade. If everything goes well, there is likely to be at least 22 different communications between firms, systems, and individuals. This ecosystem should be viewed as self-contained (for simplicity's sake for now). In other words— the CNS function, and use of an exchange between brokers is limited to brokers. Investment/Asset Managers and their clients belong to a connected, but distinct and separate ecosystem and workflow. They do not have direct access to exchanges (with some caveats), and they do not directly participate in the CNS process. Figure 2.2 details the CNS process with an example. (Box section, as Figure 2.2 CNS example)

Continuous Net Settlement

There are some great reference books specifically on the mechanics of CNS-type systems. Effectively, the way CNS systems operate is for a community of firms to all agree to use and provide funds for a central system that will facilitate the exchange of securities and cash.

All firms then submit their trades into the system as they happen. The central system then will effectively *net* all the activity throughout the day, or a set period. Take four firms independently trading stock X throughout a day as an example.

If all the transactions were settled individually, nine trades with potential interdependencies on available shares and money would need to be settled, and effectively being 18 different movements of shares and 18 movements of cash. Instead, the central counterparty inserts itself, netting all activity creating only four transactions—reducing cross-counterparty risk, as well as freeing up money and shares that would otherwise be locked up.

For example, Broker A would normally need to have 430 shares on hand to satisfy their sales, or take on risk hoping their buys would settle in time to satisfy and shortfall. Instead, they only need to have 21 shares on hand.

Enter the Manager

Brokers exist to enable access to markets by the rest of the world of firms. In this scope, I consider Investment Managers (also *Asset Managers*) as a broker's primary *client*. The Investment Manager is making decisions on how to manage their portfolio, so will instruct their broker(s) to buy and sell assets (stocks and bonds, typically). The broker, through an exchange (loosely defined), is then interacting with a broker who is working for a different Investment Manager, who may have a different investment strategy and matches the other side of the trade. Brokers do trade for their own purposes (called *proprietary* trading), but I am going to focus on trading that is a result of interaction with Investment Managers.

Let's better define our new participants, which we add to our original basic flow picture, and expand it out in Figure 2.3:

Investment (or Asset) Managers: These firms operate different kinds of investment methods. Historically, they were responsible for investing a large company's pension money, to ensure its growth for that company's employees. Today, there are many different varieties, where some managers operate their own *funds* that companies (and sometimes individuals) can participate in, and others who manage other companies' funds and investments.

Broker A	Buy	Sell	Amt	From/To	
	100.00		($99.00)	B	
		200.00	$202.00	C	
		150.00	$151.00	B	
	300.00		($299.00)	B	
	50.00		($51.00)	D	
		80.00	$75.00	C	
				Net $	Net Shs
Totals:	450.00	430.00		($21.00)	20.00

Broker B	Buy	Sell	Amt	From/To	
		100.00	$99.00	A	
	150.00		($151.00)	A	
		300.00	$299.00	A	
		350.00	$346.00	C	
		200.00	$202.00	D	
				Net $	Net Shs
Totals:	150.00	950.00		$795.00	(800.00)

Broker C	Buy	Sell	Amt	From/To	
	200.00		($202.00)	A	
		80.00	$75.00	A	
	350.00		($346.00)	B	
		140.00	$142.00	D	
				Net $	Net Shs
Totals:	550.00	220.00		($331.00)	330.00

Broker D	Buy	Sell	Amt	From/To	
		50.00	$51.00	A	
	140.00		($142.00)	C	
	200.00		($202.00)	B	
				Net $	Net Shs
Totals:	340.00	50.00		($293.00)	290.00

Figure 2.2 CNS example

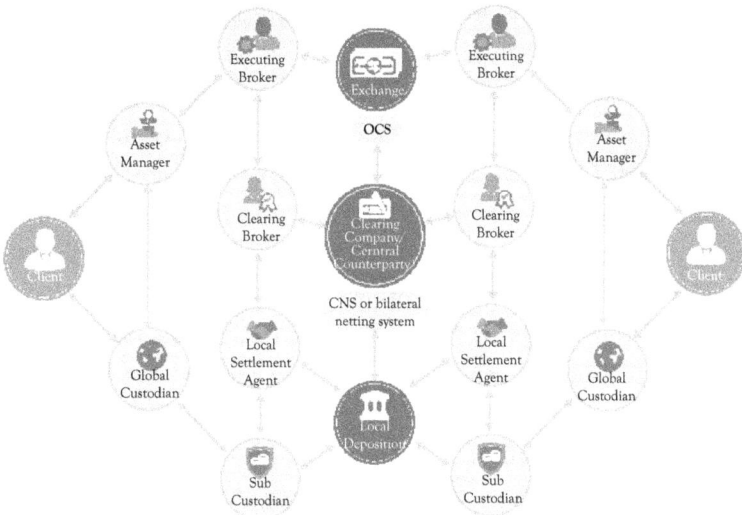

Figure 2.3 Expanded view—basic Global functional relationships

Client (may be *beneficiary*): For our discussion here, these are the firms and/or individuals who have hired the Investment Manager to manage their portfolio of assets and money. Beneficiaries typically designate their custodian, and their investment manager does not have a choice but to interact with that custodian. Beneficiaries may also manage their own investments, where the Asset Manager simply becomes an order taker.

Custodian: In most cases, the *clients* need to have a bank designated to be their record keeper, holding, and safekeeping their assets. Also could be a *Global Custodian* in the case of international investment, trading, and settlement.

Settlement Agent: In the case of a Custodian, also known as a *Sub-custodian*. This is an organization that has membership and rights in the local settlement system (typically the depository previously reviewed). The Sub-custodian maintains an account, or series of accounts at the depository on behalf of their client (the custodian).

The beneficiary (client) either instructs their manager to perform a trade, or is informed by the manager that a certain trade was done. The beneficiary then instructs the Custodian to expect this trade from the Manager. The Manager needs to inform the Custodian of the broker's information, as the settlement of the actual trade will need to occur between the Custodian (or their sub-custodian) and the broker (or their designated agent).

More intermediaries can enter the equation, especially when dealing with international markets or very specific niche markets. In Figure 2.4, we see how this can become complicated very quickly. There are a host of different providers that are specific to certain asset classes or functions, or that provide special access—like Prime Brokers or correspondent banks. There are system and platform providers that end up becoming core parts of the trade flow for managing specific information, like margin or settlement instructions. Regulation in particular markets also creates new functions or actors such as those that control entry and exit points into and out of their marketplace.

Varieties and nuances exist. Hedge Funds, while in many cases act much like an Investment Manager, typically look for the ability to directly access the market through a *Prime Broker* relationship. They are a broker that allows the hedge fund to use its name and rights to directly access markets and trade without the broker in the middle. The Prime Broker ends up looking, or acting, more like a Custodian than a Broker. Correspondent brokers may exist in small regional areas and enable access to executing brokers. And a single firm may internally collapse a group of these different functional roles together.

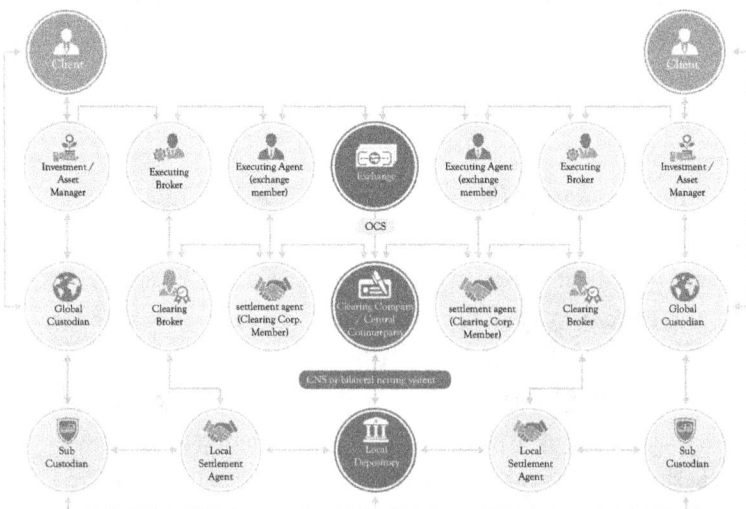

Figure 2.4 Expanded view—adding complexity

The IM Viewpoint

But as we mentioned before, the flow for an Investment Manager is distinct from the broker-to-broker-and-exchange flow we first looked at. When considering the IM viewpoint, the broker may or may not be accessing an exchange to execute. While pricing needs to follow certain rules, the broker may have shares in their proprietary *book* (or want to buy a position into their book), and therefore, do not actually access and interact with an exchange to facilitate the transaction for the IM. In this way, we can just look at the extreme left hand or extreme right hand of the illustration. At a high level, The IM agrees on details with the Broker—either at a specific price or a limit, number of shares and other assorted details.

The Details In-Between

The broker fills the IM's trade—but doesn't typically just purchase a few million shares all at once. There are many reasons for this, but let's just accept that the broker executes many trades—or has a mix of exchange trades and proprietary pieces—at many different prices throughout the day until they completely *fill* the IM's order. The broker will quote this back to the IM as an *average price*—weighting the prices at which each piece was done. This simplifies the flow between the IM and Broker, reducing the actual transactions between the parties.

At the same time, the IM is managing many portfolios, and typically will bulk up orders for a particular stock into a single order sent to a broker. After the execution is completed, the IM will then *allocate* shares out to the different beneficiary accounts across their portfolio. The broker, at this point, will need to know this allocation breakdown. One of the main reasons is that each beneficiary (or ultimate client) has a different account, and likely at different Custodian Banks. In which case, the broker needs to be sure to deliver the shares to the right Custodian for the benefit of the beneficiary—not necessarily the IM.

Following this flow, consider an Investment Manager buying shares for four clients, in Figure 2.5. Across the clients, they have 700 shares to purchase, and send that order to their broker (one).

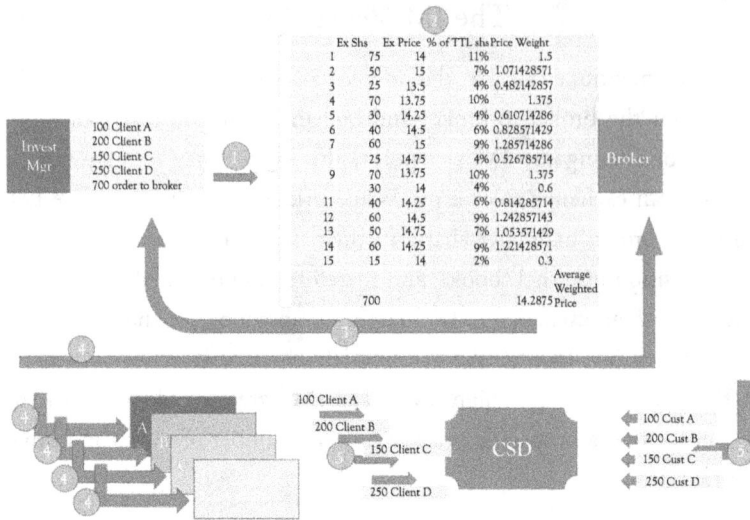

Ex Shs	Ex Price	% of TTL sha	Price Weight
1	75	14	11%	1.5
2	50	15	7%	1.071428571
3	25	13.5	4%	0.482142857
4	70	13.75	10%	1.375
5	30	14.25	4%	0.610714286
6	40	14.5	6%	0.828571429
7	60	15	9%	1.285714286
	25	14.75	4%	0.526785714
9	70	13.75	10%	1.375
	30	14	4%	0.6
11	40	14.25	6%	0.814285714
12	60	14.5	9%	1.242857143
13	50	14.75	7%	1.053571429
14	60	14.25	9%	1.221428571
15	15	14	2%	0.3

700   Average Weighted Price 14.2875

Invest Mgr

100 Client A
200 Client B
150 Client C
250 Client D
700 order to broker

Broker

CSD

100 Client A
200 Client B
150 Client C
250 Client D

100 Cust A
200 Cust B
150 Cust C
250 Cust D

Figure 2.5 Fills versus executions and average price

The broker, looking to get the best price throughout the day, works the order over 15 different executions, all at different prices and quantities (two). While the broker is dealing with matching the orders on the exchange and subsequently settling these on a net settlement basis across all their other activity with the central counterparty, the broker still needs to confirm back to the Manager that 700 shares were filled at an average price of $14.2875 per share (three). And also plan to onward deliver the actual shares to the Investment Manager. Each client of the Investment Manager, though, may use a different Custodian bank. Therefore, the Manager must confirm with the Broker that the 700 shares should be split into four different groups, with different delivery instructions (four). The Broker may or may not know who the ultimate client is. The Investment Manager must also inform each of the Custodians to expect the shares, and pay the requisite money (four). This exchange occurs outside of the central counterparty, and typically within a local depository system (Central Securities Depository). As there is no netting of activity for these transactions, successful settlement is dependent upon the delivering party actually having the shares (or bonds, or other financial instruments) in hand (five).

As the reader can hopefully see, even a simple transaction can be complex, and involve many different roles, systems, processes, and groups. It can go across countries, bringing into play different laws and implications. Each of these variations brings in different communities with different goals, interpretations, information, processes, viewpoints, and needs.

CHAPTER 3

An Introduction to Applied Linguistics

Linguistics is the scientific study of language and mainly concerns itself with describing and understanding language. It was started by the Indian scholar Pānini in the sixth century BC and formal linguistics developed in Ancient Greece and China sometime in the fourth century B.C. The many areas of study in linguistics tackle everything from meaning, semantics, and stylistics, to theories proposed by Norm Chomsky on competence and performance (individual capacity for language versus its use in different contexts and groups).

Applied linguistics take those lessons and apply them to real-world problems, from language education to translation, and further to natural language processing. Applied linguistics is focused on solving and addressing real-world issues. My focus is more toward the applied linguistics discipline so that I might address the real-world problems in financial services. "In fact, we would argue that contemporary applied linguistics is not so much a *field* as a *way of exploring*; it's a process, a 'mode of enquiry' for working with language-related problems and needs."[1] There are technical areas within Financial Services, most notably Knowledge Graphs and Ontologies, that relate more closely to applied linguistics, and for individuals involved in those areas, you will see some common themes. Indeed, the position here is that those disciplines and efforts can be further strengthened and focused through applied linguistics.

I will start with five foundational statements I will rely on as I look at financial services through an applied linguistics lens:

---

[1] Hall, C.J., P.H. Smith, and R. Wicaksono. 2011. *Mapping Applied Linguistic*, 19. New York: Routledge.

1. Communities of Practice: These are groups defined by their shared culture, functions, and processes that result in a distinct and unique language unto themselves.
2. Language is constantly evolving, and is dependent upon change and diversification.
3. There is no *right* or *wrong* language.
4. Language (and therefore data that represents language) always exists in a multitude of forms.
5. Language is a social construct, as opposed to something that can be legislated.

The theme of right or wrong language is the one around which the other four points revolve. The social construct refers to how speakers are blinded by their own view.

> We may as individuals be rather fond of our own dialect. This should not make us think, though, that it is actually any better than any other dialect. Dialects are not good or bad, nice or nasty, right or wrong—they are just different from one another, and it is the mark of a civilized society that it tolerates different dialects just as it tolerates different races, religions and sexes.[2]

I will also refer more to Charles Hockett's Design Features, especially around interchangeability, the duplication principle, and arbitrariness in regards to these five points.

Surrounding this, and directly applicable to the purpose of this book you are reading, is

> [B]elieving that governments and academies can ring-fence a language from outside influence is as naïve as believing that everyone outside the borders of Italy can be prevented from eating pizza or that everyone outside the borders of China can be forced to celebrate the new year without fireworks.[3]

---

[2] Trudgill, P. 1994. *Dialects*. Florence, KY: Ebooks Online Routledge.

[3] Hall, C.J., P.H. Smith, and R. Wicaksono. 2011. *Mapping Applied Linguistic*, 12. New York: Routledge.

AN INTRODUCTION TO APPLIED LINGUISTICS   29

Further, looking from the other direction, it is a myth that each nation has only one language.[4] This myth is a recent one born out of using language as policy to drive centralization and consolidation of power and control.[5] In recent times, there are examples of support at the state level in the United States for the restriction or banning of the use of other languages, with up to 30 states adopting English-only statutes since 1981. The motivations typically involve arguments toward the costs to local governments for providing multilingual access. The effect results in the inability of non-English speakers to participate in everything from local government to social services. Across the Atlantic, *Proper English* was particularly enforced among the London elite to ensure the ability to identify someone not from the upper class. Mincken, in The American Language, explores this extensively, where the *protectors* of *correct English* said everything about American was wrong.[6] We can look further back into 19th Century Germany, as well. German was made the dominant language of the Habsburg Empire, and the only path for social and economic advancement was to speak German. This led to even Czech-majority regions to shift to German language use and solidified a formerly haphazard collection of communities.[7] While one might argue this *standardized* language, it is easy to point out that the Czech language is still in existence, and used broadly in a cultural sense. So while power and control may appear to have been achieved, it is more that the problems that existed were simply hidden, more easily ignored, and left to fester.

It is the myth of the existence of a single language that is one of the more dangerous myths, setting easy traps for otherwise sound motivations and goals to fall into. This theme of the dangers of monolithic thinking about language, and the need to instead advocate a pluralistic approach to language in financial systems (and regulations that govern them) will continue to be a primary one throughout this text. This is not to

---

[4] Hall, C.J., P.H. Smith, and R. Wicaksono. 2011. *Mapping Applied Linguistic,* 13. New York: Routledge.

[5] Hall, C.J., P.H. Smith, and R. Wicaksono. 2011. *Mapping Applied Linguistic,* 24. New York: Routledge.

[6] Mincken, H.L. 1919. *The American Language*. Knopf.

[7] Diglossia and Power: Language Policies and Practices in 19th Century Habsburg Empire, edited by Rosita Rindler Schjerve.

dispute Chomskyan concepts of a universal grammar that ties languages together, but is advocating that there are multiple languages that exist that need to be tied together, as opposed to the assumed existence of a single monolithic financial services language.

Communities of Practice in Financial Services

"The silo mindset does not appear accidentally nor is it a coincidence that most organizations struggle with interdepartmental turf wars. When we take a deeper look at the root cause of these issues, we find that more often than not silos are the result of a conflicted leadership team."[8]

"Information silos and poor risk management have cost global banks billions… Modern systems are powerful enough to integrate functions across a bank, but often their adoption is stopped by managers who want to protect their own turf."[9]

Anyone familiar with financial services will likely nod along to these comments about silos in the industry. Silos are the bane and blame for almost any and all ills that befall the industry (and many other industries outside of finance) and are oft described in negative terms. They are an easy to conceptualize target. This is because a *silo* will typical embody very specific cultures and processes that those outside the silo would very much like to change. They would like to change them because that target culture, associated processes, and practices do not match up with the observing party's own culture, policies and practices. I posit that silos are not an evil mechanism born of turf wars and self-preservation intent on obfuscating the wrongdoings of banks from the world until they

---

[8] Gleeson, B., and M. Rozo. 2013. "The Silo Mentality: How to Break Down the Barriers." *Forbes*, October 2. https://forbes.com/sites/brentgleeson/2013/10/02/the-silo-mentality-how-to-break-down-the-barriers/#554ede888c7e (accessed January 4, 2021).

[9] Writes Gillian Tett, U.S. managing editor and columnist at the Financial Times (and author of *The Silo Effect*), Groenfeldt, T. 2015. "Silos can be Costly in Banks." *Forbes*, December 28, 2015. https://forbes.com/sites/tomgroenfeldt/2015/12/28/silos-can-be-costly-in-banks/#700ee642356f (accessed January 4, 2021).

culminate in the next Great Depression. Instead, silos are a natural phenomenon that—while certainly the source of many of the problems and market impacts—does not mean that silos are necessarily bad or should be eliminated.

"The great thing about standards is that there are so many of them!"—most often attributed to Andrew S. Tanenbaum[10] (although sometimes incorrectly attributed to Grace Hopper).

"The most damaging phrase in the language is we've always done it this way!"[11] (This is Grace Hopper.)

Tanenbaum's quote is typically said with sarcasm and derision. I would like to say that I believe there being so many standards *for the same thing* is actually a good thing (no sarcasm). Multiple standards *for the same thing* typically align with different silos. FIX, as a message protocol tends to be dominant within the *Front Office* silo while SWIFT messaging (based on ISO 15022 and ISO 20022 standards) is predominant in *Back Office* and *Payments* silos. Meanwhile, FpML is the main standard for OTC Derivatives. All functionally are communication protocols for sending information from one firm to another.

The *Silo* and Communities

The term *silo* is commonly used to refer to some system (operational, technological, or a combination of both) that is unable to (or perceived unable to) operate with other systems. This can be due to any number of forces, from technology to organizational issues and includes things like a lack of shared goals, tools, or communication pathways.

Silos are seen across industries, but are fairly pronounced within financial services. Whether it is a global operations separated from a U.S. (or other country) domestic-specific operation, or a traditional Fixed Income/Equity/Derivatives trading desk separation, silos are seen as having been created by legacy technology infrastructures, fiefdoms created

---

[10] *Most often* is, of course, a lazy way to avoid controversy, but is in his book *Computer Networks* (1981), p. 168.

[11] Hopper, R.A.G.M. March 9, 1987. in an Interview in Information Week 52.

by power-hoarding individuals, lack of organizational capability, or some other negative catalyst. The silo is blamed for a *mentality* that occurs when departments or groups do not share information, goals, tools, priorities, and processes with other groups or departments. It is blamed for negative impacts to operations, low morale, and is held up as a marker for the future failure of the business.[12] Yet, the mentality can also be the creator or at least the maintainer of the silo, making this an even more challenging problem.

I would instead argue that silos are a natural occurring phenomenon, steeped in culture and shared process, that are necessary to ensure work is done efficiently, deep knowledge is created, and an overall better result continues to be produced. This does not mean that they do not present challenges that need to be addressed and solved. There is credence to the claim of the need to *break* down walls between silos. But the approach to date has not focused on preserving the integrity of those silos, but instead on the elimination of differences in order to create some sort of operational harmony.

The result, and the prevailing go-to solution of many an enlightened leader or consulting agency, is the breakdown of silo walls. A whole industry has been defined by those silo-busting efforts, across books, *change agents* and consulting firms. The return on investment (ROI) for many is a combination of eliminating *legacy* or *duplicative* technology infrastructure, downsizing of staff (with all the positive sounding pejoratives of *doing more with less*, *strategic realignment of staff*, and so on), and gaining of *efficiencies* by being able to use the same data, and therefore, reduce errors and friction. Experience shows that as common as these *silo-busting* efforts are, so too are reversal efforts.

For example, in the 1990s, Banker's Trust looked to merge domestic and global settlement operations to simplify systems and processes. But the effort was never completed because of the amount of differences across areas like tax treatment, corporate actions, accounting, and messaging. Further back, the original global operations were actually created when the company looked to expand in 1984 and the lack of expertise in global markets was highlighted by a number of unforeseen problems.

---

[12] Roughly interpreted from the Business Dictionary

Ian Mailer Sidebar

Ian Mailer worked at Bankers Trust Company[13] "In 1984, with the purchase of WM company in Edinburgh, they planned to take custody in house in Europe from AMRO and Barclays to the Harbour side Operation, but there were numerous issues.

1. BT as a US operator, did not have a multicurrency investment system.
2. no expertise in European corporate actions or indeed Global Markets.
3. launch of the Master Trust service in Europe.
4. they attempted to use the WM accounting system as an instruction system and then manually rekey to globenet. Inefficient and costly.

It was a baptism of fire. Globenet could not cope with the fx currency matches required for settlement, resulting in a considerable loss in their first year. I actually had to go to Wall Street and sit with the exec and explain how double entry accounting on the WM system worked!!"

I have always put this down to a cultural difference and legacy market technicalities. What do I mean by that? The U.S. market was relatively simple (and all the better for it). Raising capital in Europe usually required a rights issue, a concept not practiced in the United States at the time. This was hard to explain to the U.S. operations teams. I had become WMs training officer by the time I moved to BT, so was able to try and train the U.S. corporate action (CA) team as quickly as possible. It wasn't a matter of how good the staff was, just getting them used to the way the rest of the world worked.

Another example was in the early 2000s as the Bank of New York looked to merge domestic and global settlement operations and technology for the purpose of finding efficiencies and shedding older technology and

---

[13] Ian, M. May 15, 2020. E-mail message to author.

processes. In the end, the technology just put a wrapper around the domestic system that was supposed to be *retired*—it was never integrated. This would further complicate integrating with Mellon Bank when the two companies merged a few years later.

In 2009, Barclay's acquired Lehman's equity traders, allowing Nomura to purchase the technology infrastructure around the Lehman equity trading system. The idea was that Barclays, primarily a Fixed Income house, could easily integrate equity trading into the more complex world of fixed income execution and order management systems. Among many delays, Barclays would have to build an entire equity subsystem, while the equity traders sat idle, unable to trade, for far longer than originally estimated. I attribute this to a failing in appreciation of community's differences.

In applied linguistics, a *community of practice* (CoP) is a version of a *speech community*. Typically, *Speech Communities* can be well defined through culture, idioms, and language-specific markers that can be used to define them and make them distinct from other speech communities, even if there is some overlap. CoPs are used as a bounding mechanism for applied linguistics to help define a potential speech community because they share some common culture, processes, and procedures that link them together in practice. The actual documentation of the unique speech factors that differentiate one CoP from another may not initially be known or understood at the onset, but the methodology is meant to enable that analysis from an applied linguistic perspective.

> Wegner-Trayner defines a Community of Practice as:
> A community of practice is a group of people who share a concern or a passion for something they do, and learn how to do it better as they interact regularly. This definition reflects the fundamentally social nature of human learning. It is very broad. It applies to a street gang, whose members learn how to survive in a hostile world, as well as a group of engineers who learn how to design better devices or a group of civil servants who seek to improve service to citizens.
> In all cases, the key elements are: **The domain:** members are brought together by a learning need they share (whether this shared learning need is explicit or not and whether learning is

the motivation for their coming together or a by-product of it) **The community:** their collective learning becomes a bond among them over time (experienced in various ways and thus not a source of homogeneity) **The practice:** their interactions produce resources that affect their practice (whether they engage in actual practice together or separately)[14]

In financial services, we use a number of different terms that dance around the concept of CoPs, and come from different perspectives across technology, operations, organizational structure, and business practices. Domain, Silo, Business Unit, Functional Unit, Firm type, Product type, Asset type, and similar terms all speak to a subset of financial services that is bound by a set of shared processes. These terms all speak to the same type of concept, even if the context in which they are used differ. These shared processes are typically unique, or have unique aspects that differentiate them from each other, as well as a culture that embodies the community.

As described in the prior chapter, firm type is one of these concepts that can bound a Community of Practice (i.e., *Sell side* versus *Buy side*). But communities can be overlapping, or even subsets, especially at overlapping intersection points (e.g., Buy side mid office). This complex inter-relationship is expressed in Figure 3.1.

Each of these terms infers what is embodied in a CoP; a community bounded by those shared processes (or *practice* in some linguistic circles), understanding, and culture. All of these must be in place to properly define a CoP. Belonging to one CoP, such as Equity, does not infer that there is shared understanding, practices, or culture between Buy Side and Sell side, or between Front and Back offices.

The practice is important because it identifies knowledge with something people "do" as part of their culture, profession, or avocations. (As any teacher will attest, knowing without doing

---

[14] Wegner-Trayner, E. and B. 2020. "Introduction to Communities of Practice: A Brief Overview of the Concept and It's Uses." *Wegner-traynor.com: A Partnership,* https://wenger-trayner.com/introduction-to-communities-of-practice/ (accessed January 4, 2021).

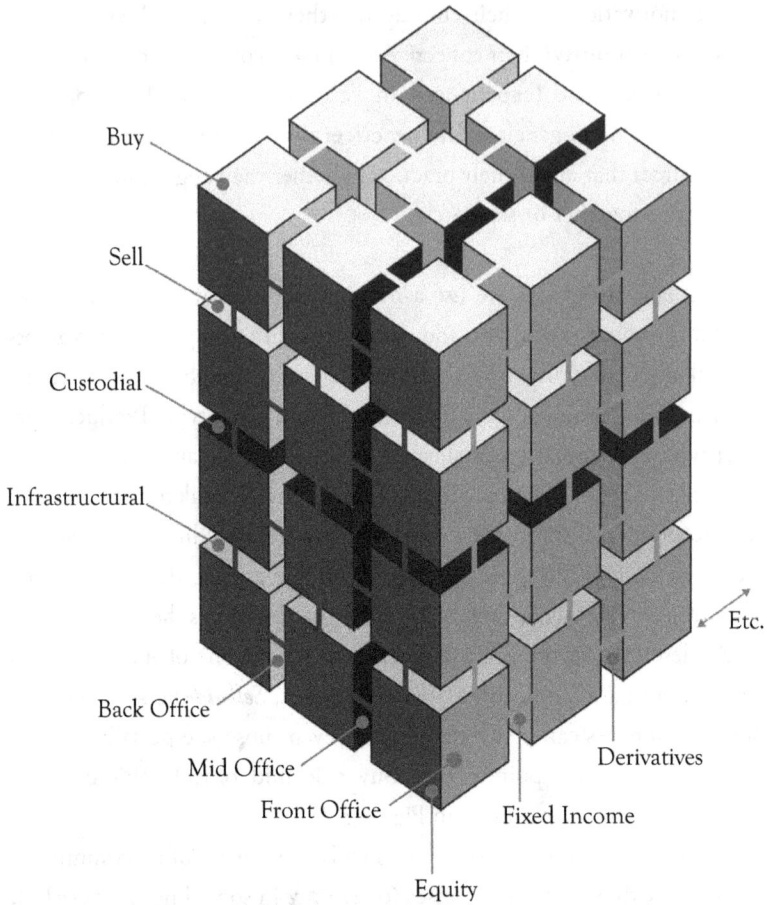

Figure 3.1 Community of practice matrix

seems nearly impossible; whatever learning residue exists rarely sticks.) And, as another key insight, Constant says a practice is not enough to specify where knowledge lives, because disconnected groups may share a practice or even a set of practices, but if they are not in contact (harkening back to the idea of a community as a group of people in communion with each other), *the meanings of those practices will not be the same.*[15]

---

[15] Hoadley, C. 2012. Chapter 12 "What is a Community of Practice and How Can We Support It?" In *Theoretical Foundations of Learning Environments*, ed. Land, S. and D. Jonassen. https://books.google.com/books?id=FJOoAgAAQ BAJ&lr= (accessed January 4, 2021).

What is important here is the distinction raised that two groups that share a practice should not be looked at in the same way—if they are not in direct shared communication or interaction, their practices (and therefore their data, language, and interpretations) will differ. Further, it is important to note that when the existence of a Community of Practice is not identified, this is not a *wrong* thing. Going back to our main tenants concerning linguistics, remember that there is not a *right* or *wrong* language, there is simply the fact that a language (a way of speaking) exists.

So, what? Within applied linguistics, the goal is not just to document the language of a CoP. Within the socio-linguistic field, the goal is to solve a problem that is linguistic-based; namely the problems in communicating across these CoPs effectively, the effective sharing of information required by multiple CoPs (adjacent or overlapping), and resolution of conflict between CoPs. Looking back at the complaints about silos, the language used to describe the issues they present center around those exact topics. Let's remember the complaints about silos. Silos are a representation of conflicted leadership teams. Silos are artificially created to *protect turf*. Silos are re-enforced by old technology that doesn't enable sharing of information. Across silos, processes are not aligned. Further, the culture of a particular silo is typically highlighted as something *not aligned* with the observing group doing the analyzing, and that it is somehow disruptive, or otherwise undesirable.

I propose, instead, to view silos as Communities of Practice. In doing so, we can view a silo through the lens of a community that shares a different culture and language than others with which it must interact. Instead of looking to *bust* silos, the effort is to be focused on enabling interoperability and language translation between differing CoPs. As I position the discussion in this way, something becomes very clear; much of the conflict between silos, or silos inside a larger organization, can be described as clashes of language and culture. As I refer back to the use of language for politics and control, another aspect of *silo busting* is the perception that the undesirable silo is somehow misbehaving, or otherwise not aligned with the analyzing group's goals. By silo-busting, the view is that power and control can be re-established through the imposition of some form of monolingualism, as opposed to approaching the problem from a multilingual perspective.

Language, Evolution, Change, and Diversification

Professor Mark Liberman (University of Pennsylvania) asks as part of an Introduction to Linguistics course: Here is a puzzle: language change is functionally disadvantageous, in that it hinders communication, and it is also negatively evaluated by socially dominant groups. Nevertheless it is a universal fact of human history.[16] When I sit back and think about this, language change does seem counter-intuitive. The existence of the thousands of languages globally that exist introduce friction into communication and make it difficult to interact as human populations.

This language change doesn't only happen among your large traditional languages like Japanese, German, or English. Populations that speak the same language also will drift apart when separated. In isolated subpopulations speaking the same language, most changes will not be shared [between subpopulations]. As a result, each subgroup will drift apart linguistically, and eventually will not be able to understand one another.[17]

In traditional human language, changes are affected by such things as learning (one language expert teaching someone new to the language), contact (communication and interaction between groups that differ in language and dialect), culture (societal concepts and norms, from dress to beliefs), and natural use that results in such things as slang or change of meaning. Further, language continues to diverge toward multilingualism as opposed to monolingualism.

> This is all the more true as the focus has shifted from Europe's allegedly monolingual and monocultural national states to a global view, showing that most people cannot live their everyday lives without making use of several linguistic varieties. It seems that multilingualism by far outweighs monolingualism, measured on a historical and global scale (cf. Ludi 1996), an assumption that becomes even more convincing if we accept that there is no

---

[16] Liberman, M. n.d. "Linguistics 001 Lecture 22 Language Change." *Introduction to Linguistics* Syllabus. https://ling.upenn.edu/courses/Fall_2003/ling001/language_change.html (accessed January 4, 2021).

[17] Liberman, M. n.d. "Linguistics 001 Lecture 22 Language Change." *Introduction to Linguistics* Syllabus. https://ling.upenn.edu/courses/Fall_2003/ling001/language_change.html (accessed January 4, 2021).

straightforward distinction between multilingualism and multi-lectalism.[18]

Simplistically, bringing together communities of different languages and agreeing on an overall governance does not unify those communities into a single language, or overrule the continued existence of the underlying communities or CoPs. Relating this to the financial services community, the larger community can be viewed in the lens of multilateralism; it is more of an alliance of multiple Communities of Practice pursuing a goal of an overall functioning within an interconnected financial system. Being an instance of multilateralism, and not a specifically distinct community on its own, the nuances and differentiated data and speech between CoPs in the alliance would not and do not lose distinction. This is consistent with human language.

> [T]he general tendency seems to be for the dialects on both sides of a political border to become more and more dissimilar, that is, to diverge. This tendency is in conformity with the "proximity principle" discussed above. Internally, however, state borders tend to have unifying effects, although the linguistic unification is never absolute (cf. Sapir 1921: 213 fn.). This finding, too, is in keeping with the proximity principle. In short, convergence on the dimension of dialect to Standard language and of dialect to dialect (i.e., linguistic unification within state boundaries) necessarily leads to divergence at the borders. Thus political borders that transgress old dialect continua are turning into new dialect borders.[19]

---

[18] Kuhl, K.S. Hoder, and K. Barunmuller, eds. *Stability and Divergence in Language Contact: Factors and Mechanisms.* Studies in language variation, volume 16. John Benjamins Publishing Company. https://books.google.com/books?id=CKtgBQAAQBAJ&printsec=frontcover#v=onepage&q&f=false (accessed January 2021).

[19] Hinskens, F., J.L. Kallen, and J. Taeldeman. n.d. "Merging and Drifting Apart. Convergence and Divergence of Dialects Across Political Borders, International Journal of the Sociology of Language." no. 145 https://degruyter.com/view/j/ijsl.2000.issue-145/ijsl.2000.145.1/ijsl.2000.145.1.xml (accessed January 2020).

Relating the various Communities of Practice within financial services to states bound by political borders, it should follow that even when there is some shared language, dialect borders exist and will define where divergence will continue to grow.

Right Versus *Wrong* Language

"Languages often have alternative expressions for the same thing ('car' and 'auto'), and a given word can carry different senses ('river bank' vs. 'savings bank') or function as different parts of speech ('to steal'—verb; 'a steal'—noun). Because languages naturally adapt to their situations of use and also reflect the social identities of their speakers, linguistic variation is inevitable and natural.

So what is right and wrong in language, and who decides? Some observers claim that the real issue about linguistic right and wrong is one of deciding who wields power and who doesn't."[20] This idea of power is one that should be of keen interest to those involved with financial services. Especially post 2008, regulators around the world have begun to flex their muscle to bring greater stability, fairness, and access into the financial system. (I do note the seeming lack of focus on optimization, function, and positive outcome regarding the purpose of the financial system's existence in the first place, however).

One of the more subtly impactful actions, and one that I believe does not garner enough attention, is the focus on the creation or standardization of a common financial language. In December 2017, the European Commission launched a public consultation that refers to the development of a common financial language (European Commission 2017). The Commission's Financial Data Standardisation (FDS) project also refers to the lack of a common financial language (European Commission 2016, p. 11). This subject was once again raised at the EU Commission Conference "Preparing supervisory reporting for the digital age," which was held in Brussels on June 4, 2018 (https://bit.ly/2J5TA0R). And it is

---

[20] Edward, F. 2020. "What is 'Correct' Language?" *Linguistics Society of America.* https://linguisticsociety.org/resource/what-correct-language (accessed February 2020).

also represented in the expansive work that has been conducted on the Global Legal Entity Identifier since 2008 as well as in the efforts of the U.S. Office of Financial Research (OFR), which was formed as a result of the Dodd–Frank Act.

In the context of linguistics, it can be observed that various regulators are deciding what is right and wrong in financial services language through the exertion of their given power. Further, this viewpoint toward requiring a common financial language has parallels to the concepts of *language as a problem* (Ruíz, R.).[21]

> The specific outcomes for students is that they are blamed for failing by implying that they are not smart enough, motivated, or appreciate the educational opportunities the school system gives them (Darder 2011). This is deficit thinking by "blaming the victim" (Ryan 1971). These programs stemming from deficit thinking, show bad results worldwide, and assimilate children while at the same time prevent them from getting a good education (Cummins 2001).[22]

We can relate students in this examination to the various CoPs and actors within the financial system, and regulators to the powers looking for a monolinguistic financial society. The various CoPs are looked at as deficient because of their individual languages, processes, and cultures. Deficit thinking, and the belief that CoPs intentionally behave badly, and primarily use their individual languages to prevent transparency and understanding, simply reinforce regulators' collective view for the need to force change in all CoPs to a monolinguistic reporting and operational scheme. There seems to be a view that various CoPs intentionally create their own language in order to obfuscate and prevent outside observation and understanding. And therefore that this language is somehow *wrong*. Meanwhile, as we identified previously regarding change, linguistics tells

[21] Ruíz, R. 1984. "Orientations in Language Planning." *NABE Journal* 8, pp. 15–34. Doi:10.1080/08855072.1984.10668464

[22] Harrison, G. 2007. "Language as a Problem, a Right or a Resource?: A Study of How Bilingual Practitioners See Language Policy Being Enacted in Social Work." *Journal of Social Work* 7. Doi:10.1177/1468017307075990

us that this view is most likely incorrect and the truth is in line with the simple fact that language evolves and diverges, especially within CoPs, with clear distinction at their borders.

Multitude of Forms

According to Wittgenstein's **use theory of meaning**, words are not defined by reference to the objects they designate, nor by the mental representations one might associate with them, but by how they are used. For example, this means there is no need to postulate that there is something called *good* that exists independently of any good deed.[23]

> Meaning-in-context, on the other hand, is less static and more elusive. The meaning of an utterance requires an understanding of its context, a familiarity with the way the utterance is being exchanged, the intention of the utterance, and the position of the utterance within a 'language game' or 'conversation'. Such a theory of meaning must take into account that the subject is a creative, imaginative agent who extends (or projects) new language practices from prior encounters, and that such meaning is framed by the individual's social and discourse practices.[24]

What we can indicate here is that a word may differ in meaning based on use and context, data and language in financial services is also subject to a multitude of forms, based upon the CoP that generates that data or language. The same *data* (i.e., *word*) generated by two different CoPs not only may, but most likely will, have different meanings. These meanings necessarily will be dependent upon the context within the CoP; how and why it is being exchanged or generated, and where in the process specific to that CoP it is being used.

---

[23] "Ludwig Wittgenstein" *Stanford Encyclopedia of Philosophy.* https://plato.stanford.edu/entries/wittgenstein/ (accessed January 4, 2021).

[24] Brace, E. 2014. "Referring to Wittgenstein's Later Theory of Meaning; Understanding the Relationship Between the Form, Meaning and Use of Language." https://theliteracybug.com/meaning-form (accessed May 2020).

For example, I want to identify IBM Common stock. If I use a ticker code, that infers IBM common stock in a certain context—namely on the particular exchange or data platform from which that ticker originates. Meanwhile, use of another code, say a SEDOL, also refers to IBM Common stock, but specifically to the settlement regime or clearing regime in which it exists. It is now devoid of the nuances of exchange or data platforms, and ignorant of other clearing and settlement regimes in which IBM common stock may also exist. Yet, in response, if I require use of an ISIN code, which would uniquely and specifically indicate only IBM common stock, I lose the nuances of either exchange or clearing and settlement regimes. The individual objects may be the *same*, but at the same time, they are very different. And therefore, their meaning and intentions also differ.

Language as a Social Construct

Language, and data that is created in that language, are created by people in order to facilitate communication. They do not exist *naturally*, but are instead *constructed* by the social group, the community, that requires the language to communicate information and accomplish its goals. While this may seem obvious, or a simple aside, the implications are important when speaking of Communities of Practice, and the language that is specific to that CoP. As a social construct, language, and the objects they describe, are bound conceptually by the CoP defining them. Multitude of forms and arbitrariness exist partly because language is a social construct, is defined by and evolves subject to a specific CoP's influence and use.

In Hockett's design principles, this relates to cultural transmission, in which language is learned through the social setting. While humans are born with innate language capabilities, the expression of concepts are learned, and are a part of learning. The other implication of this is the language that is used by two different CoPs will differ based on the needs and purpose for which that language is used. This is as much a point in understanding not just the language, but the social context in which it comes from.

A Nod Toward Infology

Infology comes from the work of Börje Langefors, a Swedish engineer and computer scientist. As part of his work, he formulated an *infological equation* noted as I = I(D, S, t), which describes the difference between data and information. The mathematical expression captures an observation that *I*, *Information*, communicated in an information system is a function (*i*) of the data *D*, the semantic background *S*, and the time interval of the communication, *t*.[25]

Infology and Decentralization

Information systems theory has, since its beginning in the early 1960s, been facing a contradiction. One of its main visions was that data in the system had to be available to "everybody" (Langefors 1961, #29, 1963, #37). But it was soon detected that a set of data does not inform everybody (the "infological equation." Langefors 1966, #1). It had to be concluded that efficiently designed information systems had to be structured as a network of communicating more or less separate subsystems based on local data systems. This insight took a surprisingly long time to gain recognition in the data profession, as well as, for instance, in accounting.

Even when, in the 1980s, small local systems came to be fairly common, this was in many cases due to the emergence of inexpensive micro-computers, rather than to an understanding of the often local character of data. [26]

What Langefors indicates with the infological equation, and in the aforementioned conclusions, is that local data has its own character, and should be connected into the larger system in a way that preserves its local nature. However, he notes that this *truth* about data was not recognized. While some may point to the 1980's decentralization effects, they were

---

[25] Langefors, B. 1966. *Theoretical Analysis of Information Systems*, 197. Lund, Studentlitteratur.

[26] Langefors, B. 1995. *Essays on Infology*, 159. Chartwell-Bratt.

not intentional in the means of acknowledging the local character of data. Indeed, centralization continued and continues today to be a major theme and objective in technology and organizations.

Like Machine Learning (ML) and Artificial Intelligence (AI) in 2020, the work of Business Information Systems was, and continues to be focused on using data to provide useful insights (information) that can be communicated to others. The contradiction here is that information systems, including today's ML and AI, focus on making sure that everybody can access ALL data, while the point is made that some of that data "does not inform everybody." In other words, there are data that, based on the time period of the data and the *semantic background*, does not need to, nor should be, exposed to *everybody*. This is, of course, structured in the view of computer science, and the mechanisms of technology. But we can relate this to our Communities of Practice easily. The *semantic background* and the concept of *local data* are both analogous to a specific CoP. In other words, there is local data specific to a community (the *semantic background*) that doesn't necessarily have meaning or utility for everybody.

From a pure information systems perspective, subsystems typically perform very specific tasks. They can be specialized and only relevant for niche processes. Therefore, this means that the local data can conflict with or is not relevant to other systems, either because those other systems aggregate data irrelevant to processes the local system is performing, or the other systems only *care* about a subset of the data generated by any local subsystem.

This is expressed further:
And, with the maturing of the technology of connecting small computers to form networks, one has begun again to talk about making all data accessible to everybody. We conclude that there is still lacking the understanding that some data are only intelligible to restricted groups of people. This suggests that there is need for case studies, in order to reach and disseminate a more concrete understanding of this aspect.
It is often stated, e.g.[,] by data managers, that the popping up of isolated local systems will lead to chaos. Leaving aside the fact that some

amount of chaos may be useful, we point out that keeping isolated such data as are in in any case unintelligible outside a limited context can't by itself generate chaos. Of course, such data as [sic] have to be used in several locations, but those only, must be subject to integrated management—but this should not be done indiscriminately.[27]

This viewpoint in infology provides the same conceptual structure and reasoning as CoPs. It recognizes that there are local systems, ostensibly dedicated to restricted groups of people for their use—a direct corollary to a CoP. Further, there is understanding that at many times, data will be unintelligible to other people and systems—just as a different language would be between isolated or otherwise contained CoPs. And as with any information system, especially as we look to ML and AI, there is the counter force of wanting to link everything and everybody and provide universal access to all data. But Infology indicates that *local data* should not be included indiscriminately, and only after *integrated management*—that is, *translation*.

Infology, expressed as information being the intersection of data and knowledge, does seem to start down the path we have taken regarding community of practice-focused attentions. However, coming more from a purely mathematical and technical focus, the underlying problem I am looking to address has never really been solved in infology. The debate over centralized and decentralized databases speaks to this continued friction and lack of resolution. Langefors here pays difference to "some data are only intelligible to restricted groups of people," but indicates that the area is largely unexplored, and instead the focus continues to be on the technical integration and information availability. The issue with focusing on technical integration and information availability is that the nuance of the S in the infological equation is typically de-emphasized, and there is a presumption that technology, applied correctly, can solve all problems.

Technology forges ahead without understanding that some data is not meant for everyone, primarily because it is unintelligible and irrelevant.

---

[27] Langefors, B. 1995. *Essays on Infology*, 159. Chartwell-Bratt. found via "Centralized versus Decentralized Information systems: A Historical Flashback." Hugoson, M.A. Jönköping International Business School, Sweden, https://link. springer.com/content/pdf/10.1007%2F978-3-642-03757-3_11.pdf

Chaos is more likely to spread in these systems by including this data instead of understanding why it should be separate. The fear is that chaos will be caused by continuous and spontaneous creation of local systems— called *shadow technology*, *dark systems*, or *rogue systems*, and that this is a bad thing, as it introduces challenges of management, risk, miscommunication, and data loss. Which are all valid points. But again, I point to the fact that language is always evolving. Many times these systems are simply instantiations of that evolution. It is hard to manage and thus the easier method is prevention instead of understanding and evolution.

Accommodation and Fixing

Accommodation and Fixing are tools within linguistics that are used to facilitate dialogue. Simply, when two speakers from different CoPs, languages, or dialects interact, there is expected to be some level of misunderstanding or lack of understanding. In some cases, the speaker or the listener may *accommodate* the other, able to process non-native concepts or words by self-interpreting the meaning.

For example, a Queen's English speaker talking to an American may say "I had to wear my jumper because it was chilly today." The American, not familiar with the word *jumper* may infer, through both language context and a clue, such as the person pointing to their sweater as they spoke, that *jumper* means *sweater*. Further, they do not *call out* or otherwise question this. Meanwhile, the English speaker may instead use the word *sweater* instead of *jumper*, knowing that it may introduce confusion, and thus, accommodates the American speaker. Finally, the American speaker may reply back and use the word *jumper* instead of *sweater* in future speech, therefore accommodating their British friend.

Fixing, on the other hand, would involve initiating a query, acknowledging a break in understanding, and resolving that misunderstanding. This is a feedback and repair mechanism. In our previous example, the American may not have had enough context to interpret *jumper*. Instead, they would ask outright "what is a jumper?" and even perhaps provide their definition of what they thought a jumper was—either a set of jumper cables for a car, or a person on a ledge. A back and forth may occur, until both speakers understand that *jumper* and *sweater* are conceptually the same object.

Communication across language barriers must encompass accommodation and fixing in order to solve problems in language and understanding. Translation does not always capture these nuances either, which impacts the ability for technology to consistently solve for such cross-CoP issues. Understanding a second language natively can typically provide a better understanding than a translation from an interpreter. Each new party in the translation introduces their own biases on what may be emphasized or how it is interpreted without the necessary *fixing* occurring. Much like the childhood game of *telephone*, where a message is passed down a chain, without any corrective action, and inevitably ends up a distortion of the original message.

The problem of Fixing from a technological perspective is based in trying to fix data misunderstandings across different CoPs, especially when it is assumed that the language is shared and the same. Technology, unless it is expressly told, will not catch language nuance between CoPs in many cases. That is not to say it is not impossible—but without a specific focus and understanding of CoPs and defining them, this task will be haphazard at best, and trying to go off imperfect clues.

Further, capturing the instances of accommodation, especially where members of certain CoPs are naturally multi-lingual, is a larger challenge. There will be cases where users add in extra information automatically to make deductive leaps in regards to accommodating clients and counterparties from different CoPs. While NLP, ML, and AI can get very good within a specific language to ask questions regarding fixing, accommodation is a next level concern.

Wrap these two issues underneath the prevailing assumption that there is, or should only be, one 'financial language' and technology has no guide in performing either of these tasks. Technology solutions will gravitate toward a bias for whichever CoP it is most used by, and re-enforce the conflicts and misunderstandings that exist between CoPs when that technology interacts with those that do not share its bias.

CHAPTER 4

Intermission

There are many terms that get used interchangeably. Some of these conveniences are OK, and some are not.[1] For any one role, there are as many nuances to that role as there are varieties of salmon. Take traders as an example. There are sales traders, execution traders, and so on. And a trader can also be a broker. Brokers are market makers and include institutional, middle market, bond dealers, and bond brokers. Not to mention, the term *broker* may refer to an individual or a firm!

If we are talking in general terms, it is less of an issue if such terms are generalized or interchanged. One example of how this can become problematic would be the qualifications and regulatory requirements that may be attached to or inferred by one term over another. In general, brokers tend to deal with individual investors directly, while traders execute on behalf of firms and salespeople. For example, a trader does not (and cannot) act as a salesperson. In the United States, they must pass the Series 57 Exam from Finra whereas brokers must take the Series 7. This distinction is important in the operational functioning of a trading desk, as well as its composition and regulatory compliance. But, depending on where you sit and the level of your interactions with a trading desk, the distinctions could introduce unnecessary complexity and noise, making it perfectly fine to use generalized terms. In most cases, this does not present an issue, except when the specialized knowledge intersects with a particular impact resulting in misunderstandings and confusion. For example, if a derivatives trader is asked for a price, they typically will give a percentage representing the yield they are locking in, but if the asking party is from operations, they are likely looking for the dollar per

---

[1] With apologies to my true linguistics experts, who would rightly argue that an individual's use of a term in a way that someone perceives as *wrong* is actually OK, in the spirit that there is no *wrong* or *right* in language.

unit. Without being more specific about the type of price or how it is expressed, this will introduce unnecessary back-and-forth, even though they are both talking about *price*.

The further away from direct interaction one may be from a function, the more likely you are to gloss over nuances, or even outright ignore significant differences between concepts. This relates directly to the previous section on subject matter expertise. For the majority of the population, it is simply impractical to expect anyone to be able to have a deep level of understanding further beyond their direct realm of contact. And even if there is previous experience, over time that knowledge may become stale or otherwise skewed. What is the point here? That the details matter. What is important is to remain aware of that distinction—and understand that some details might be missing and might matter—before you hang your hat on any final viewpoint. Stay aware of context and community. We know this, as humans, but tend to readily ignore it. "The shoe is on the other foot" and similar phrases are common expressions that speak to perspective mattering—and how an opinion can change depending on where you stand (i.e., the *community* to which you belong). What is viewed as the *right* answer or interpretation depends on the details—both surrounding the questions, as well as the backgrounds and knowledge of those observing. And more importantly—the lack of knowledge and awareness (or lack of awareness) of these contexts.

Over the next several chapters, I will explore different Communities of Practice—the groups defined as silos, domains, among other differentiating terms. Each chapter will take a different lens, viewing the industry from different perspectives that end up giving us different slices, or viewpoints to what is a shared community. There are plenty of books and reference materials that go into the specific roles and functions of the various market participants. What I will try to express is perspective and viewpoint, more so than function and basic block-and-tackle processes such as *step 1, to step 2 to step 3* basics.

I will be presenting some basic Communities of Practice that exist in financial services. My goal is to present the CoP, and contrast them with other CoPs—why they are different through their culture, processes and procedures, function, relationships, perceptions, and so forth. CoPs are fluid, as are any speech community. They may overlap, or have boundaries that are a bit fuzzy at the edges, as illustrated in Chapter 2. And while one CoP may have a common culture, that does not preclude individuals in that CoP from sharing a culture with and belonging to a different CoP at the same time.

CHAPTER 5

Firm Type: Perspectives, Roles, and Languages

The *Buy Side*

To define the buy side, I look to the *sell side* as they are best defined in opposition. Where the sell side is generally set up to enable raising of capital for other firms through issuing debt, equity, and other investment options, the *buy side* roughly equates to those that are buying those investment opportunities, and therefore funding the market (with the expectation that their investment will grow and make more money, of course!). Note that in Mergers and Acquisitions, *buy side* refers to the investment banks working for potential buyers of a firm, while sell side is the investment bank working for the selling firm. From a general financial services perspective, both of these investment banks are *sell side* institutions! To add to the confusion, investment *banks* are sell side, while investment *managers* are buy-side.

So, the role of the buy side is to invest money. Where does this money come from? There are institutional investors and retail investors, with a somewhat loosely defined *middle market* of investors. Most institutional investors we are familiar with are firms and governments that have pension funds or other retirement options for employees. Other kinds of investors are insurance companies, endowments, and foundations. Retail investors can be high net worth individuals, or your regular person with a personal retirement or other kinds of investment accounts. Small businesses and home offices sometimes are considered retail, but sometimes get put into a *middle market* segment, as they may have significantly more money to invest than any one individual, but nothing on par with a state government's pension fund. Also, some high net worth individuals get lumped into the *middle market* depending on the size of their net worth. Overall, there are different kinds of mutual funds, exchange traded funds, hedge funds, private equity funds, in addition to individual stocks and bonds.

What Can You Buy—Why Funds?

Stocks and bonds are the basics in investing. Individual investors can buy individual stocks and bonds. Meanwhile *funds* are basically a mixed basket of different stocks and bonds. The benefit being that the need to research different stocks and bonds is reduced, and an investor can *own* a much greater variety of companies. This is meant to reduce the risk an investor may take on any single company stock, although the potential reward can be less, as well. An investor may buy 100 Pets.com stocks and miss out on Amazon because they don't have enough money to spread around. Also, they are taking a chance that they are picking companies that will perform well. Meanwhile, a fund may invest in a wider variety, meaning any *losers* won't impact the overall performance of the fund.

The buy side is comprised of many different flavors of firms. Some operate their own funds, while some firms contract out to professionals and invest their client's money with many different funds. But they all share the same goal—see the money they invest grow through the increased value of those investments, or through returns paid directly via interest payments or dividends. The language of the buy side focuses around clients as those investing money, and who are the ultimate beneficial owners. Brokers and the *sell side* are counterparties. Custodian banks are service providers, many times as forced relationships directed by clients that have a preference for one or more custodians. The buy side is focused on performance for the client, and understanding the different needs, from ERISA (Employee Retirement Security Act)—restricted investors to private equity investors.

A Buy-Side Manager's direct universe in the trade process consists of their clients (those with money looking for help and advice investing that money), counterparties (the broker/dealers), service providers (custodial banks, 3rd party lenders, payment processors) and information service providers (data vendors and communication platform providers). At a very basic level, the manager has a portfolio of different assets (a mix of stocks, bonds, derivatives, and so on) that they are trying to optimize to align with a particular strategy of investing. This could be based on risk (high risk, low risk), tracking an industry group (industrial, technology), environmentally conscious investing (ESG), income or growth (lots of dividends and cash payments versus simple value growth), or any combination of these. The first consideration is whether money is coming in to invest, or if a client is taking money out. This requires the portfolio manager to make a decision on what to buy or sell, while maintaining their strategy and balance. The portfolio manager, once they know what they want to do, works with their trader (or trading team) to execute the appropriate orders (buy/sell instruments). The trader will be given parameters on target prices and volume. The trader will use various means to find broker/dealers (and yes, potentially other venues—more on that later) to buy or sell the securities they are working on. Depending on the asset type, this can be done via phone calls, broker-provided screens, communication intermediaries like Bloomberg, and so on.

At a very high level, an investment manager will have different funds, where each fund is focused on some goal or investment strategy. Some examples would be investing only in bonds, or a mix of bonds in a specific percentage classified as *high yield* versus higher quality. Or it may be based on industry sector—such as a fund investing only in technology stocks, or a mix of *green* companies. Alongside this, the investment manager will be selecting different funds for clients to invest in, across a portfolio of investments to match the client's risk appetite and goals. So, on day to day, an investment manager will be looking at the performance of funds, and portfolios, measured against expected goals and outcomes. If a fund is supposed to have a specific mix in value of different investment types, and this mix becomes substantially out of balance, the investment manager may need to *rebalance*, which is typically done at specific intervals. In the same vein, if a client portfolio becomes unbalanced to their goals or risk appetite, the investment manager would look to buy or sell investments to bring it back in line. At this point, the investment manager would need to record the pending trade in their systems, in order to enable a number of processes. If selling securities, shares need to be *locked* so they aren't oversold. If buying, there needs to be enough cash in the account, as well as on-hand. There are other transactions going on as well, so the cash balance may not reflect what the balance will be in the future. Compliance checks begin to be run to make sure the trade doesn't violate any thresholds. The investment manager would contact a broker/dealer and initiate the buy or sale. They would already have an account in place with that broker/dealer, sometimes at the direction of the underlying client. In any case, the investment manager would first express interest in buying or selling. The broker would respond with their current *best bid* price. If the price is acceptable to the investment manager, they would authorize the broker to proceed with the sale.

So, in defining the Buy Side as a Community of Practice, we would need to recognize their purpose, their goals, as looking to serve the needs of investors (and profit from that), yet rely upon interaction with those that can access the financial markets, and provide services required for attaining their primary goals. Information they collect is aimed toward those goals, as is the bias of the data they output. Their language is focused around the investments and how to communicate primarily with those they serve—the investors, rather than those that provide them services.

The *Sell Side*

As described before, the sell side is generally set up to enable raising of capital for other firms through issuing debt, equity, and other investment options. Additionally, the sell side provides access to markets for purposes of financing and investing available capital. There tends to be high specialization in the sell side, as the process for raising of capital is distinctly different from the subsequent secondary market of investment, and the corresponding operations that support these distinct processes. Further, sell side tend to become specialists and experts—necessary to provide the depth of knowledge their counterparts on the buy side rely on to make informed decisions (i.e., where the issues of paying for research originated). All these factors help define the Community of Practice of the Sell Side.

The sell side is usually what the average person thinks of when *Wall Street* is invoked. Given the amount of money involved, and the impact to the economy, especially the role played in almost every depression and recession in the modern era, the suspicion that all of the sell side look like Michael Douglas (of Gordon Gekko *Wall Street* fame) walking around saying "Greed is Good" is well earned. But for every Long Term Capital and "Wolf of Wall Street," there are thousands of events, deals, and transactions that occur day to day without such intrigue. However, these Hollywood views of *Wall Street* help give a window into the culture, one of the factors in defining the bounds around this CoP. Flamboyant, risk taking, aggressive—all things people may associate with the moniker *sales*.

There are, generally, three main sides to the Sell-side; the investment banking, secondary markets, and principle/proprietary business. While they all work together, there is good differentiation that results in different goals and focus. Research also is a major role for the sell side, though with a bit more separation from the markets/trading areas.

Investment Banking

Investment Banking focuses on deal making and the raising of capital—either through debt and/or equity offerings, or other investment options. Investment Banks, operating alone or in a syndicate (usually based on the size of the deal), facilitate the underwriting, contracts, generation of investment interest, and so on. While the *IPO* (Initial Public Offering) attracts a lot of public attention, many times the day to day ranges from municipal bond offerings for your local school district to bonds offering to finance a firm's expansion. After the *dealmaking* and the bonds or stocks are *in the marketplace*, these instruments are available for the general public to buy and sell in the *secondary market*. In the investment banking function, the sell side are essentially facilitators, same as the Dutch financiers from all those years ago. Brokers can also perform related functions, which will be explored a little later in the context of the differing and contrasting CoPs that are involved. Prime Brokerage, Correspondent, Clearing, and other functions give unique views within a single broker firm that may perform opposing functions.

The Capital raising portion of the sell side has a number of specific structures and processes that support its needs. Companies or other entities (like a school district) that wish to raise capital either work with a single investment bank, or a group of investment banks in what is known as a syndicate.

The investment banks, in this role, structure the deal, and handle registration with the appropriate regulatory agencies. They then communicate these offerings to trading desks, perform initial offerings and settlement, manage outstanding instruments during the offer period, buy any of the left over offerings, and set the date for trading to commence.

Secondary Trading

A significant amount of activity with the buy side occurs in the secondary market. In most cases, the buy side is looking to establish long-term viability and growth in its investments. This is not gained through investing primarily in IPOs and early stage companies—but instead in established firms with proven track records. The secondary market is composed of the type of trading done in the world's stock exchanges, where shares of companies are available to the public to buy and sell, as opposed to shares that are privately held by an individual or group. Similarly, most of the fixed income and corporate financing is in instruments that have traded hands already and are being bought and sold after their initial offering. Hence, the *secondary* market.

Again, here the sell side are acting as facilitators—enabling the public access to markets and investments, and providing expertise. Related services come out of this activity, such as research and sales. Research is where the broker provides their clients with information they gather about investments. It is not considered *advice* but instead a service where the broker has a more direct connection to news in the marketplace, especially about different new offerings that may be coming, or trends in the industry based on mathematical models the broker has developed.

Principle/Proprietary Business

At the same time, brokerage firms are investing their own money (the *proprietary book*). Brokerage firms have their own profits to invest, which are kept separate from any trading decision making involving clients.

The principle business has roughly the same goals as any *buy side*—invest, hedge bet, and grow money. Much of the original proprietary business activity came about from the activities of supporting the investment banking function—as part of facilitating a deal, the investment bank takes on the risk and provides funding, or underwriting, of the deal with the expectation that this will be a temporary *loan* until it is purchased in the marketplace as the initial offering.

To protect any exposure, the broker would invest in other investments that would provide some level of *protection* if the investment made in the original deal failed. In contrast to a typical *buy side* investment, however, proprietary trading was necessarily shorter term. The sell side, by the nature of being a financier, needs quick access to funds, so it is unable to *tie up* money in longer-term investments. This need for ready cash needs to be balanced against having large sums of money sitting *unused*.

Further, short term investing provided a way for the sell side to take advantage of movements in the markets to make extra cash, where otherwise the money would sit unused. So, even outside of hedging risks of the investment banking activities, *prop trading* became a significant portion of a broker's activities, with its own risk management functions, and a major part of a broker in its own right. Up to the late 20th century, brokerage firms were primarily structured as *partnerships*.

The *resting cash*, in essence represents the partner's savings. Having it sit around idle while they enabled investment for the rest of the world and not using their knowledge to increase their own money wouldn't make sense. Upon retirement, a partner would take the value of their investment with them, so there was motivation to generate as much profit from idle cash as possible. This has shrunk significantly over time as the largest firms transitioned from partnerships to public companies and either bought, or were bought, by other firms. The business was further curtailed due to regulations, particularly the Dodd-Frank Act in 2014, which restricted most short term investments.

From a Community of Practice perspective, then, the Sell Side is focused on the generation of capital (money), and the language and data is particularly biased toward this. However, as necessary, the Sell Side needs to serve the needs of the Buy Side.

Custodians, Sub Custodians, and Local Agents

The role of a custodian bank has changed little over the years, even while they have grown to incorporate other services. An investor needs a firm to manage their books and records, and custody (hence, *Custodian*) their assets. An investor will chose the custodian bank they use for their books and records. They will then direct their investment manager, and give the manager the authority to work with that custodian on their behalf. As previously covered, the investor may or may not be managing their own money. Here, we will assume the investor has a relationship with an investment manager. Depending on the size of the investor's portfolio, they may have more than one investment manager, and may elect to use more than one custodian. To keep things simple, we will deal with a singular relationship on all sides. Effectively, this larger community of custodians can be broken down into the individual roles of Global, local, and subagent communities.

A Custodian performs multiple functions, from accounting, to supervising functions such as cash management, corporate actions, risk management, post-trade compliance, securities lending, pricing, and valuation. Global Custodians (GC) are contracted to enable investors with global holdings. In this way, the investor and manager only have to deal with a single entity, regardless of whether they are trading in New York, London, Hong Kong, Sao Paulo, Tokyo, or South Africa. A global custodian will establish a network of relationships with other custodian banks that are located and registered in specific markets. Some global custodians have their own extensive network, and have their own branches in each country. Most still establish a subcustody relationship with a local bank, especially in smaller and emerging markets where establishing their own branch may be prohibited by cost or regulation. The subcustodian's relationship is directly with the global custodian, and in many cases, the subcustodian has no direct knowledge of the investor.

Local Agents are in most ways like subcustodians. However, the term *local agent* is typically only associated with custodian type banks in a local market that are servicing a global broker or sell side firm. The services required by a sell-side firm are different than those of a buy-side firm, from regulatory and reporting requirements to different cash services and accounting. The local agents and subcustodians are the banks that belong directly to the specific market's depository or central registry for securities settlements and cash payments. These firms are at least one step removed from the initial transaction and the actual transaction they are handling is typically only a piece of a larger set.

On the securities settlement side, after an IM has executed a trade with a broker, they will allocate, and break up the fully executed amount across the different client investor accounts they are managing. Each account at this point is treated individually, as each client account can have a corresponding account at a specific, possibly different, global custodian. The IM will need to send an instruction to the GC, informing them to expect to deliver or receive securities in the referenced investor's account in exchange for cash, with a specific broker, in a particular market. The GC will then send this on to the local market sub custodian, and manage the status, ensuring that there is enough cash or securities on hand for the projected settlement day, and that any local market matching that is required prior to settlement is performed by the sub custodian.

Fiduciary Duty

ERISA Section 3(21)(A)(i) specifically defines a fiduciary as anyone to the extent: "he exercises any discretionary authority or discretionary control respecting management of such plan or exercises any authority or control respecting management or disposition of its assets[1]

In many cases, this defines the difference between a Trustee and a 'simple' custodian. However, even for non-ERISA accounts, there is argument that there is an element of fiduciary duty for custodians to their clients. In the 1990s, as an Investment Assistant at Bankers Trust Company, I handled a large volume of transactions. Not all of them settled properly—due to errors ranging from shares not being available, wrong instructions or account numbers (see sidebar on omnibus accounts), not enough cash, or a myriad of other reasons.

---

[1] "29 CFR § 2510.3-21—Definition of 'Fiduciary.'" 2020. Cornell Law School, Legal Information Institute. https://law.cornell.edu/cfr/text/29/2510.3-21 (accessed January 4, 2021)

Fails in settlement carried penalties—many times borne by the broker counterparties—and thus they were highly motivated to make sure trades settled. But, sometimes, the client had a fundamental disagreement with what was actually transacted; anything from the price per share, to the commission and fees, to even the currency, and country that the trade was settling in could also be in dispute.

When this happened I would receive phone calls from these brokers sometimes calmly, sometimes not, explaining why I needed to change my client's instructions to get the trade to settle and how my client was wrong. In this case, I held no fiduciary duty to the broker, but I did have a duty to the client to follow their instructions, not those of their counterparty.

Once a broker tracked down your phone number in the back office, though, you were guaranteed to get frustrated, and sometimes threatening, calls, claiming financial ruin. If you were doing your job, though, you were already in contact with your client, and they were fully aware of the fail, and the reasons why.

While this seems like a very simple process, there are a number of related concerns. An account may have a *base currency* rule where all cash is expected to be exchanged into a specific currency. There may be special accounting needs. Deliveries may be dependent upon incoming receives, and shares may need to be borrowed to handle shortfalls. There may be particular rules or extraordinary events (strikes, work stoppages, etc.) in a specific market or country, and the global custodian is expected to know these, the impact to the investor, and ensure any instructions or trades coming from the IM comply. There are also rules on segregating certain accounts from others, and managing inventories in co-mingled accounts. Depending on the asset class, other functions may be needed. Derivative positions require management of collateral and margin calculation, cash requires short term investing,

On the IM side, the GC will provide them with settlement instructions for each account. When the IM confirms their allocations with the broker, they will need to provide the broker with this information. The broker then will need to send instructions, including the settlement instructions, to their local agent. The local agent and the sub custodian then contact each other through their local market conventions, make sure the corresponding details (which they have received from their respective clients) agree, and prepare the stages for local settlement. The local agents and subcustodians are expected to be experts in their market. While the Global Custodian needs to understand each individual market, the local service providers provide the on-the-ground market interaction. Figure 5.1 provides an overview of the different services Global Custodians provide to different communities.

Industry Infrastructure and Utilities

Industry infrastructure and utilities come in a variety of flavors. From an operational point of view, these institutions typically service a singular purpose in satisfying the needs of a specific community, usually by reducing risk or performing a commoditized shared function for a market. The primary infrastructures in most developed markets are typically Central Counterparties (CCP's), Central [securities] Depositories (CSD's), exchanges and related venues, payments processors, and secure messaging facilities.

CCPs, as discussed in Chapter 1, provide a risk-reduction facility— both through reducing the trade and money that must move, and through operating a contingency fund in case one of the participants becomes insolvent. CCPs can exist solely for cash-type transactions (like CLS), or for different financial instruments (stocks, bonds, etc.). In the traditional construct, firms pay to be members of the CCP, and the CCP uses those funds to guarantee settlement of agreed transactions between those members. CCPs typically agree to accept this risk from particular exchange(s) or venue(s), which then requires participants' clearing parties to belong to the CCP. CCP's members tend to be brokerage-type firms, as these are the primary members of the exchanges that look to utilize CCPs for the risk reduction and market protection.

CSDs provide central books and records for a particular market. In typical cases, all eligible securities are deposited at the CSD. This can mean the actual eligible physical stock or bond certificates, in which case they are held in physical form in a vault, or more advanced markets have

TYPICAL GLOBAL
CUSTODIAN SERVICES

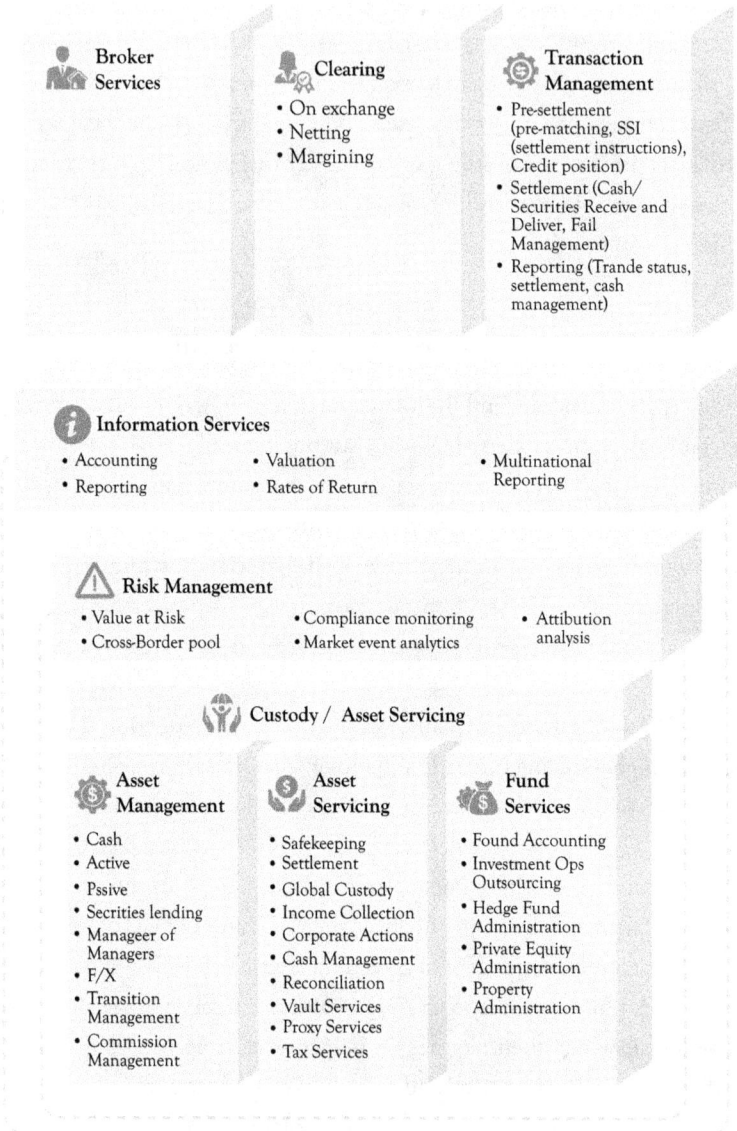

Broker Services

Clearing
- On exchange
- Netting
- Margining

Transaction Management
- Pre-settlement (pre-matching, SSI (settlement instructions), Credit position)
- Settlement (Cash/ Securities Receive and Deliver, Fail Management)
- Reporting (Trande status, settlement, cash management)

(i) Information Services
- Accounting
- Reporting
- Valuation
- Rates of Return
- Multinational Reporting

⚠ Risk Management
- Value at Risk
- Cross-Border pool
- Compliance monitoring
- Market event analytics
- Attribution analysis

Custody / Asset Servicing

Asset Management
- Cash
- Active
- Pssive
- Secrities lending
- Manageer of Managers
- F/X
- Transition Management
- Commission Management

Asset Servicing
- Safekeeping
- Settlement
- Global Custody
- Income Collection
- Corporate Actions
- Cash Management
- Reconciliation
- Vault Services
- Proxy Services
- Tax Services

Fund Services
- Found Accounting
- Investment Ops Outsourcing
- Hedge Fund Administration
- Private Equity Administration
- Property Administration

Figure 5.1 Custodian services

dematerialized all eligible securities and now they only exist as digital records. In either case, the CSD is responsible for maintaining who is the *holder of record*—which may or may not be the actual beneficial owner.

This is because the custodian banks that hold the account and relationship with the CSD may operate what is known as *omnibus* accounts, which may hold inventory of many clients together.

Omnibus

A global custodian deals with multiple clients. Traditionally, before computers, all stocks and bonds were physical paper certificates. Ledgers kept track of who owned what, but typically, as long as you had a physical certificate that was properly endorsed to you, that overruled any other recordkeeping.

The exchange of actual paper when buying and selling eventually led to bottlenecks and efforts were made globally to dematerialize securities.

At the same time, as the number of investors grew, this meant individual accounts for each one, and in many cases, for each individual portfolio, which exponentially multiplied the number of accounts. As discussed previously, Global Custodians contract with different local custodians in individual countries to handle responsibilities requiring local presence. Opening individual accounts at each of these local agents multiplied the difficulties of tracking all these account numbers.

An *omnibus* account was the answer. A Global Custodian could open a single account to house all the securities and cash for all their clients. The Global Custodian would do the management of who owned what in their own sub-accounting records, and the local custodians would not need to worry about different account numbers when trying to perform settlements and other functions. This greatly simplified management of hundreds of thousands of individual portfolio accounts.

The real requirement, however, was to make sure that when there were multiple deliveries and receipts in a single day, the correct account owner was credited or debited the share and/or cash involved. If two clients had deliveries, for example, and one client had the shares in their account, while the other was depending on an incoming receipt to cover the delivery, there had to be assurances [for] the client who had the inventory settled, even if the pending receipt didn't come in.

Partly due to this, certain markets still required that an account be opened for each individual owner ('beneficiary account'). Sometimes multiple portfolios for the same client could reside in a single beneficiary account. Further, certain types of accounts, like regulated ERISA accounts required 'segregation'—to ensure their inventory was never bundled with other kinds of non-permissible inventory, such as higher risk assets, that could put the omnibus inventory at risk.

While individual, segregated accounts for every individual beneficiary would be the 'safest' and most transparent method, it carries high costs. Additionally, there is a greater chance of a settlement failing due to data errors, as counterparties would need to track all these thousands of account numbers on an individual client level, as opposed to just a handful based on a Global Custodian's omnibus. Given the number of parties involved in a transaction, the risk of errors increases greatly, even with automated processing.

International CSDs operate essentially as intermediaries between clearing parties and local market CSDs, where the clearing firm does not need to belong to the local CSD. Originally, they came about to enable CSD-like functions for *stateless* or multijurisdictional instruments, like Eurobonds that spanned multiple EU countries. The lines have blurred further as Euroclear acquired local CSDs, such as France's Sicovam (among others) and the reverse occurred when Clearstream was acquired by Deutshe Borse, the German CSD. Additionally, regulation such as TARGET2 Securities further complicated the CSD view, at least in Europe. Under TARGET2 Securities, it effectively opened up the requirement that any trade in any European Union country would be settled through a single platform, regardless of the specific CSD.[2]

Exchange

The definition of an *exchange* has been stretched over the years, with the advent of *alternative venues*—although modern alternative venues date back to the late 1960s with the emergence of AutEx

---

[2] European Central Bank. 2009. *"Settling Without Borders"* https://ecb.europa.eu/pub/pdf/other/settlingwithoutborders_t2sbrochure112009en.pdf (accessed January 4, 2021).

and Instinet. More recently, Multi-Lateral Trading Facilities (MTFs) and Swap Execution Facilities (SEFs) and even inter-dealer broker systems have blurred the lines of what an *exchange* implies. Strictly speaking, and as defined in the regulations, an *exchange* refers primarily to formal stock exchanges that existed prior to the 1960s alternative venues. They are organized under specific regulatory rules that are required to be met to be licensed in the particular jurisdiction in which they operate, and for the asset classes they list and enable trades.

Linguistically, we could argue that *exchange* encompasses all of these constructs—in the act that they facilitate the exchange and trading of financial instruments, although how they accomplish this function (and sometimes for what purpose) has a great deal of impact on the type of regulation a particular marketplace may impose on the different instances (whether it is a *traditional* exchange, or an MTF, SEF, or even some *systemic internalizer*).

Types of Venues

As stated, until recently, the concept of an *exchange* or *venue* was mostly uniform and formalized. Exchanges, like the Amsterdam Stock Exchange or the New York Stock Exchange are places, or venues, where a broker can meet with other brokers (either in person or via technology) to agree to buy and sell financial instruments. Exchanges are typically regulated markets, and offer more than just a location to trade between brokers, chiefly around listing (*initial public offerings*) and other services. They also typically revolve around equity type instruments like common stock.

Electronic Communication Networks (ECNs) came into existence in 1969 with the formation of Instinet. This created a new type of venue, known in some regulations at *Alternative Trading Systems* (ATS) or Networks (ATNs). Technology driven, they operate outside, and alongside, formal Exchanges. Some of these also qualify as *Dark Pools*— where the buyers and sellers are not revealed to the outside, and orders are systemically matched. This allows firms to place large orders without revealing their strategies or intentions to the market and competitors that may try to take advantage.

Multilateral Trading Facilities (MTFs) sit somewhere in between, and is a European regulatory designation. In some cases, these MTF's provide IPO-like listing services, and may be operated by a single investment bank. They tend to expand outside of simple common stock and specialize into FX products, commodities, and other investments. Organized Trading Facilities (OTFs) pick up around here, dealing more in derivatives and cash bonds.

The prime benefits of these systems were faster execution, lower per trade costs, and better pricing. Their creation drove competition to exchanges, keeping them honest, as well as created more liquidity in the marketplace, despite the arguments that fragmented liquidity caused other problems and costs. ECNs, MTFs, OTFs, ATSs, and ATNs are all similar kinds of organized facilities that provide alternatives to the more *formal* legacy Stock Exchange type systems and venues. In the aftermath of 2008, European regulation sought to ensure that these venues provided more transparency to the market so investors were not disadvantaged. This led the European regulators to also look at a practice known as *internalization*.

Brokers, as discussed, take orders from clients. They can fill these from their proprietary inventory or go to one of the aforementioned venues. But doing so incurs transaction fees. They realized that with the number of clients they serviced, they could have one client buying and another selling. As long as they provided proper services in putting those two orders against each other (satisfying rules around best price compared to the prevailing markets on both the buy and sell), they could simply satisfy those orders by *systemically internalizing* them. European regulators considered this activity on par with any of the other *public* venues, exchanges and facilities, and formally designated *systemic internalizers* (SI) as a *market* requiring regulatory oversight. There are arguments on either side of this interpretation, and if the extra costs involved in extra reporting and regulation outweighs any benefits to transparency, especially since internalized trades still had to be reported. In some cases, investment banks acting as SIs converted their operations to MTFs. The function of internalization was meant to save both the broker and their clients' money on the transactions. The regulation, in effect, eliminated those savings and imposed further costs.

Infrastructure and Utilities

Infrastructure and utilities can be government regulated and mandated. This is because in many cases, these infrastructures and utilities perform specific and critical market functions for a significant portion of the economy. Just as the Custodian community is subsegmented so too does industry infrastructure have clear community subgroups. CSDs and CCPs may perform similar functions, but the communities they serve are decidedly different, and have very different requirements and needs. Infrastructure and utilities comprise functions that aim to create efficiency for the community involved in a specific activity, or related sets of activities. Stock exchanges, as discussed, provide a central location for the listing and interchange of stocks. Central Counterparties (CCP's) insert themselves between global activity to reduce risk, either in cash or stocks or both. Real Time Gross Settlement (RTGS) systems enable real time transfer of funds among participating banks in various currencies. While typically dealing in a single currency, and a function of the Central Bank, there are also utilities like CLS that provide centralized foreign exchange settlements.

However, because of their critical position in the market, there are risks of creation of government-imposed and even de facto monopolies. While many operate under a not-for-profit banner, the principles of cost recovery are not routinely followed. Where oversight of these organizations fall outside the realm of direct regulatory oversight, and even in cases where they may be deemed Self Regulating Organizations (SRO's), the opportunity for monopoly abuse, anti-competitive behavior, and the resulting stifling of innovation is significant.

Service Providers

Whereas *industry infrastructure* (i.e., infrastructure and utilities) may be viewed more as an integral and almost required piece of a certain market's financial system, service providers tend to exist just outside this integrated system. Yet, they also provide critical components necessary for properly functioning markets and processing. Also, in contrast to industry infrastructure, there is a tendency for there to be more competition among service providers—or at least the theoretical possibility of competition, less direct regulatory oversight (but not always significantly so), a more profit-driven and market driven viewpoint, and an impression that the services are a *value add*. This differentiates a service provider from a buy side or sell side firm. Custody and Treasury servicers (the Global Custodian community) sometimes are referred to as service providers. However, in the context we discuss here, Custodians are a required part of the ecosystem.

Some service providers may provide specialized functions that are also performed by others in the primary ecosystem. For example, there are providers that do specialized securities lending or collateral management, even though Custodians typically offer these functions as core services in custody. Or, a service provider identifies a function that can be *outsourced*. Many times, buy side and sell side firms need to do things unrelated to their *core* functions. These can be regulatory requirements, like trade reporting, core technology from data management to trading and order management systems, or operations support. To increase the confusion, sometimes these service providers can actually be a buy side, sell side, custodian, or utility firm. However, the function they are providing is not in their primary offerings.

Investment Management Outsourcing, for example, is an offering by some of the larger Global Custodians. In this service, the provider actually 'lifts out' the back office operations of an Investment Manager and operates it on the IM's behalf. By doing this for multiple investment managers, the service provider reaches economies of scale and efficiency that the IM theoretically could not do so on their own, and at a lower cost.

Consulting companies also provide outsourcing solutions, *offshoring* to less expensive locations when there are highly manual tasks that require larger staff numbers. In many cases, service providers offer advanced niche technology solutions, such as for reconciliation, or matching and compression of outstanding derivatives. Firms with a similar problem may come together to form a consortium, or an innovative start-up may create an automated solution that would have been difficult for any single firm to develop.

Consortiums can be an option for certain *industry infrastructure* functions, such as communication networks like SWIFT. Although not an essential network, it does provide unique and critical functionality some would consider mandatory. Others are sold by their initial consortium once they reach a critical mass, or are merged or sold to firms with similar aligning functionality, such as the history of Swapswire and Markit. Fund Administrators, Third Party Lenders, data providers, matching platforms, and communication networks are some of the types of service providers that are typically not considered *formal* financial firms. However, they provide critical services to the industry and focus on specific problem areas, such as providing aggregated data and analytics, middleware for connecting different systems, or validation services to help automate resolution of disagreements in trade details to further STP.

In the context of communities and language, service providers demonstrate broad variety. On one hand, some serve many different communities, and tend to be generalists and translators, much like Global Custodians. However, a large majority are niche providers, and therefore, have very specialized language and culture. In some cases, a single firm may have even created their own niche, and therefore, its own unique language and culture that diverges greatly from other communities.

CHAPTER 6

Front/Middle/Back Office/Enterprise (Silo Versus Cross-Silo)

Function is another way the industry participants differentiate and segment themselves into communities. When viewing the financial process, there are groupings of activities that take place in a fairly linear manner. Very roughly, this is typically viewed in three major groupings: Front Office, Mid Office, and Back Office. Whether it is preparing for securities trading and settlement, or looking at funding within a corporate cash desk, these three broad categories capture the primary CoPs generalized in financial services. We can add to this an *Enterprise* view for those functions that sit across these communities and view a firm from a holistic viewpoint. It should be noted that these community groupings exist both at an overall financial services sector, as well as within individual firms who may have two or more of the communities operating within their walls.

The Front Office CoP

The *front office* can be seen as the group that faces off against clients and counterparties and tends to *drive the bus*. The front office is comprised of brokers and investment manager trading desks, exchanges, and any connecting infrastructures. Portfolio management and execution management, and the interactions, roles, and functions performed by these make up what is typically considered the *front office*. Referring back to what most laymen envision when invoking the term *Wall Street*, it is the Front Office that captures the imagination. The upfront investment decision making and those supporting activities that encompasses much of the negotiation, sales, and analysis comprises the community that is the front office.

As this is the area where investments are made, the front office is generally the main profit center for firms that operate within this community, or have a division that operates in this community. From an investor's perspective, front office decisions either make money, or lose money, based on a number of factors. Whether it's simple stock value increases, or more elaborate betting like shorts, derivatives, or other more complex linked outcomes, the primary purpose is (typically) to increase the value of an investment.

In the front office of the sell side the traders are trying to invest and increase value for the proprietary side of their business and making money via commissions for providing trading services to the buy side—whether it be on execution, research, or even cash and securities lending services. Investment banks take fees for initial public offerings or bond issuances, as well as being market makers in the new stocks or bonds if they sell well.

In general, though, the majority of the money-making activity that embodies Wall Street *wheeling and dealing* is viewed to be within the front office. And the culture usually aligns with this—high paying jobs, high stress, risk taking, tense negotiations, quick decision making, and all that comes with it. The Hollywood movies may not be entirely accurate or fair in their treatment of the front office, but there is no denying that there is a significant aspect of that culture regardless of the firm and location.

The Mid Office CoP

The mid office is the community that supports the front office, typically aggregating, fact checking, and preparing things for *back office consumption*. It acts as an information filter and highlighter of information that flows back to front and that may impact trading, investment decisions, and cash flows. The mid office consists mainly of investment managers and brokerage firms. But most of the role of the mid offices are replete with verification of the details provided by the front office. This requires a great deal of data aggregation, interaction with multiple internal divisions, and communication with external parties. There has been a trend throughout the 2000s for Investment Managers to outsource the majority of mid office functions to service providers, for the most part operated by Global Custodians.

Internally, mid offices make accounting and transaction entries that affect books and records. Compliance checks are done. Cash projections and stock availability is calculated and evaluated. Collateral and margin requirements are calculated and acted upon. Middle office also communicates with the back office to verify and confirm settlements and to update any failing settlements that require their attention. Externally, mid offices perform trade matching, which involves verifying that the trade information they received from the front office matches what is expected by the counterparties and clients. Breaks need to be corrected, either by verifying with the front office or instructing the counterparty or client to revise their information.

The Back Office CoP

The back office is the next *link in the chain* after the mid office. While the mid office tends to verify, correct, and aggregate on behalf of the front office, the back office takes the output from the mid office and advances the transaction lifecycle. In the securities world, back office functions are sometimes broken out into two functions called *asset servicing* and *settlement*. There is a typical association of the *back office* inferring the Custodian Bank CoP and the settlement processes. While there is heavy overlap between the *back office* community and custodian bank communities, there are differences. Back office includes more participants than just custodian banks, and custodian banks themselves are not limited to just back office functions.

The back office typically begins after trade and counterparties details have been verified. This information is then passed on to effect settlement. The settlement process involves many parties, processes, and data. Many times, matching at a local level—either at the local CSD or between sub agents—is performed to identify pending settlements that may have issues, even in light of all the verification already done by the mid office. The asset servicing functions tend to expand outside the pure settlement function. Back offices track cash balances, notification of corporate actions, processing of dividends, taxes and reclaims, position management, tax reporting, safekeeping, proxy voting, and income processing. In contrast to the front office CoP, the back office tends to be more risk adverse, less well funded (being viewed as a cost center), and individuals less flashy or aggressive.

The Enterprise CoP

Previously, I have covered functions that are directly related to the initiation, execution, handling, settlement, and servicing of trading or exchanging assets between firms, and the actual interactions that take place in the market. However, there are support functions that are necessary across all of these steps that don't directly have any hand in the functioning of financial markets. These we can view as communities of their own, based around the functions they perform. While they are quite necessary and critical, we are not going to dive too deep. It is important to at least provide some examples to help illustrate how they differ as individual Communities of Practice—within individual firms, and across and overlapping other Communities of Practice.

Human Resources is an obvious community. Integral to the functioning of any firm, HR professionals have no hand (typically) in any of the financial investment functions relevant for our purposes. HR professionals have their own language and culture that is distinct from the rest of a firm. Accounting at a firm level (as opposed to as a service for clients around their portfolios and investments) is also a function that is *walled off* from the main activities of a financial firm. While *financial* in nature, firm-level accounting is more focused on high level performance and metrics than on the decision making day to day around investments.

Risk and compliance, in contrast to the previous two examples, tend to be much more integrated into the daily life of investing. However, many times these sit alongside—as oversight, as a gatekeeper, overall policy maker—as opposed to dealing with the intricacies of settlement, or trade matching. Very much involved in ensuring compliance with legal requirements, and protection of the firm from known and unknown risks, the culture and focus of risk and compliance is sometimes viewed in opposition to the trading and operations sides of firms.

Technology and data are critical to the day to day workings of financial firms. And while it is helpful for technologists and data managers to *understand* those they are building systems for, it is not typically a requirement. Technologies and data practitioners being unique communities outside of the day to day is one of the reasons this book is needed. The differences between how these support groups interpret the needs, functions, and day to day of the different financial services communities they serve often results in systems errors, data disconnects, broken analytics, and a host of other issues that need to be addressed from a linguistic perspective.

CHAPTER 7

Asset Class CoPs

Typically, the classification of an asset type is driven by the organization and the groups that end up being responsible for managing those investments. Or, in the case of an investment manager's portfolio, the strategy behind that portfolio. Seen broadly, there are five main categories of asset classes; equity, fixed income, foreign exchange, commodities, and derivatives and each has a distinctive aspect. This is simply one view, however, and where any particular financial instrument gets classified, it can vary depending on who is doing the classification.

While there are legal, risk, and other differences between equity and fixed income, the primary difference is the underlying premise of the instrument. Equities like stock give the holder an ownership of a firm that issued the stock. Fixed income, in contrast, represent a loan that the investor is giving to the firm, and is being repaid over time. As such, fixed income instruments have different types of data, like yields, interest or coupon payments, maturities, and tenors. In contrast, stock is primarily viewed in number of shares and price per share. Foreign exchange concerns only currency and cash holdings, while commodities involve transactions in *hard assets* like oranges, gas, oil, and lumber. Derivatives are contracts that derive their value from any one of these other kinds of assets—either as insurance against potential losses made in investments (like Credit Default Swaps), or protection against large volatile swings in currency rates when trading foreign exchange (Interest Rate Swaps). The differentiation between communities based on asset class is fairly clear owing to the different data, purpose, and processes unique to each, though there are some concepts that tend to bend the base concept of an asset class with a function that is being performed such as collateral or securities lending, and these will be further explored next.

Equity would seem to be the most consistent of the asset classes, although on the fringes, there is some muddiness. Listed futures and options (*listed derivatives*) are sometimes classified under equity. American and Global Depository Receipts (ADRs and GDRs) act more like fixed income or a derivative that are convertible into actual equity. Some would classify convertible bonds (fixed income that is convertible into equity shares) as equity throughout, while others would manage them strictly as fixed income. Preferred shares sometimes act more like fixed income instruments, but are still functionally equity in their legal definition.

Commodities (typically futures contracts on things such as oil or agricultural products) are often considered their own asset class. Given their unique properties, they are generally kept separate rather than being lumped into derivatives. They represent the oldest asset class, going back to seed merchants, and unlike the other asset classes, represent actual physical goods.

Fixed income quickly becomes segmented; such as by maturity (short term, medium, or long term), by investment type (municipal, corporate, government, etc.), risk profile (high yield vs. investment grade), and more. A quick Internet search for *bond types* illustrates this by bringing up results as varied as "The 7 types of bonds,"[1] "10 most common types of bonds,"[2] and even "All the 21 Types of Bonds."[3] The Financial Industry Regulatory Authority (FINRA), meanwhile, lists eight of the "most common types of bonds"[4] on its website. Regardless of the type of fixed income, all share some common themes such as splitting across government and corporate issuers. It serves to help illustrate that even within a specific community (be it asset class, function or firm type) that may be viewed as homogenous from the outside, there can be striking, and fairly significant

---

[1] Stanton, E.R. 1998. "Types of Bonds: 7 Bond Types Explained." *The Street*. https://thestreet.com/markets/rates-and-bonds/the-different-kinds-of-bonds-229831

[2] 2020. "10 Most Common Types of Bonds—Which Of Them Is Best For You?" *The Smart Investor*. https://infoforinvestors.com/academy/bonds/types-of-bonds/ (accessed July 2020).

[3] Borad, S.B. June 2020. "Bonds and their Types," *Sources of Finance*. https://efinancemanagement.com/sources-of-finance/bonds-and-their-types

[4] FINRA. June 2020. "Type of Bonds." https://finra.org/investors/learn-to-invest/types-investments/bonds/types-of-bonds

differences that result in clearly delineated and separate Communities of Practice.

In foreign exchange, there are splits between securities-associated needs and pure *payments* and cash management needs. While they have interdependencies, the communities are very distinct with very different goals and viewpoints. In essence, Foreign Exchange (F/X) represents trading in cash and currencies around the world.

Finally, derivatives are financial instruments based on some other asset. Many times they look like *bets* on a future state. Options, for example, give an investor the right to buy or sell a stock at a certain price in the future—essentially making a bet that the price will not be as good as what the option provides, and therefore getting a *deal*. As alluded to previously, derivatives' main function is to reduce risk of other trades. So, if a firm is worried about the value of a stock declining too much in the future, they can set a bottom limit they are willing to accept as a loss, and sell an option at that price in the future. They may not realize as much *upside* but they protect themselves from a significant *downside*. Many firms specialize in derivatives, and some even trade exclusively in them, as opposed to using them purely for risk mitigation.

The Equity CoP

Equity is accessible and the most visible asset class. Information is easily consumed by novices and experienced alike. The stock markets, stock prices, and companies' public decisions revolve mainly around the information related to the equity markets. Equity practitioners participate in an information-rich, automated environment. While poor data and many nuance-based exceptions prevent complete and true automation, it is a reasonable statement to say that equity, in general, is likely the most advanced in technology and automated processing. There is no extreme specialization within equity, as an asset type, aside from different types of exchange traded funds, mutual funds, and single stock. This is not to say that equity is simple and free of nuances and does not requires specialist experience.

From an investment type, value is easily tracked, for the most part, by liquid markets reporting prices and price changes down to nanoseconds.

Investors, and the portfolio managers catering to those investors, focus on growth, long term stability, or cash dividends as primary strategies. There is also focus on individual company performance, or how well an industry sector (such as technology) is doing on aggregate to ensure stock prices continue to increase, or dividends increase.

From a trading basis, information is readily available publicly from exchanges, and trading prices and valuations are typically standard and relatively easy to come by for all participants. Post trade, there is a robust network for confirming trade and settlement details. Multiple providers exist in ancillary services, such as securities lending, matching, settlement instructions, and counterparty interaction.

In most markets, equity is settled at a central depository (CSD), where the shares are *held*—typically as digital records. Most physical stock certificates have been *dematerialized* and now only exist as digital records. In this way, there are usually not actual physical movement, but only books and records entries based on standard secure messaging protocols.

The Fixed Income CoP

Fixed income tends to be a much more varied and robust asset class in terms of types and variety, as well as processes. From segmentation across asset type like governments, municipals, and corporate debt to differentiation across terms—short, medium, and long term, fixed income presents the need for a variety of expertise, many times resulting in highly specific specialization. Fixed income traditionally has been seen as the safe haven to place money when the stock market (equities) are not doing well, or there is uncertainty. While the post 2008 environment has changed some of the long-held rules around the correlation between equity and fixed income markets, for the purposes of community definition, it provides an initial insight into a difference in thinking about investing between the equity and fixed income communities. Fixed income, as an asset class, is based on notional value versus yields—basically the stated value at a particular time, and the interest over a stated period of time (the term) that the fixed income instrument promises to deliver. This is a very different model and way of thinking than equity, which ends up being a combination of factors related to the real time activities of a company, and can tend to be much less predictable over time.

Short term debt many times bleeds into funding and money management as a facility to invest large sums of cash that would otherwise sit idle, but still needs to remain highly liquid (i.e., available within a short period of time to satisfy any possible sudden cash needs such as a shortfall). Meanwhile, long term debt—especially *safe* government issued debt like Treasuries—is used as a safe haven for the medium to long term either to protect against volatility in the equity markets or to have long term predictable income from the paid interest. Long term debt can also be used in place of cash as collateral to finance certain activities, much like an individual may use real estate as collateral for a loan, because that long term debt is considered *stable*. In this way, a firm can use actual cash for other business and still is able to collect interest on the long term debt.

Another factor in fixed income is quality. Debt that is considered *risky* (i.e., the company has a higher probability of not paying the interest or defaulting on the principle amount) used to be called *junk bonds* and have lower ratings than debt that is not considered risky. In the current environment, high risk debt is usually called *high yield*—referring to the higher interest these types of debt instruments must pay in order to attract investment. The different quality of debt is a factor in who invests in it, and why, especially in regards to risks investors wish to take, and the reason they are investing in debt.

The contrast of the fixed income community versus equity should already be seen; the terms we have used to talk about fixed income (notional, yield, term, interest rate, etc.) are not ones used in describing the equity community. Further, the processes involved in how trading is done has even greater contrast. Where equity is traded via exchanges and venues, fixed income is traded via a *request for quote* (RFQ) methodology.[5] What this means is that the *buy side*, when interested in buying or selling a fixed income position, will contact different *sell side* firms and request a quote. This is basically the broker trader asking what kind of deal they will give for a specific amount of fixed income.

---

[5] Again, we should point out that nothing is *absolute*. Not all equity trades on venues, and not all fixed income is RFQ.

This can involve a good amount of negotiation between buy side trader and sell side trader, although there are automated systems in place that collect indicative quotes from many different sell side firms, providing the buy side some intelligence about the current range of prices for more actively traded instruments. But, at its core, each individual trade is a negotiated price different from other trades. A broker could sell the same amount of the same bonds to two different clients (counterparties), at different prices and commissions. Meanwhile, unless the markets are moving particularly fast, the difference in prices two different clients would get on an equity trade is likely to have much less variance.

At a high level, it all does look the same—traders are buying and selling, middle office is comparing details, back office is handling settlements and processes like corporate actions. But the content and context used to accomplish those functions vary so significantly that placing an equity trader on a fixed income desk would likely be disastrous, albeit a bit entertaining in a very slapstick fashion. The skills, the type of interactions, and downstream impacts create the basis for a different world view between equity and fixed income practitioners, and therefore, is the basis of a different community of practice.

The Foreign Exchange CoP

The FX community focuses on the interchange of different currencies. Within the FX community, it is bifurcated between functions related to pure cash management at a *treasury* function level versus *securities servicing* and what is required specifically in enabling the trading, settlement, and related functions around investing in equity, fixed income, commodities, and derivatives.

Corporate cash management looks at funding across an enterprise, for all functions. The trading funding is only a part of this. Funding is required for payroll in different locations, payment of invoices, taxes, and operational costs—from leases and real estate to office supplies. Cash reserves also must be maintained. This requires corporate cash managers and the FX traders to look to foreign exchange, understand and hedge for risks through forwards, anticipate shortfalls in various currencies, and move cash accordingly.

At the same time, general trading and settlement—for a firm's proprietary accounts or for clients need to also ensure cash is in place to satisfy pending settlements. For Custodian Banks and other providers, they must keep aware of clients' accounts for potential overdrafts and, depending on services they are contracted for, make the appropriate funding decisions. In cases where omnibus accounts, as opposed to individual segregated accounts, are used, ensuring the right client's funds are attributed to any trades or cash receipts or payment is essential.

As a community, foreign exchange behave very differently from equity and fixed income. Money moves rapidly, and there are no real formal exchanges. Where equity and fixed income transactions occur and then may settle days later, FX occurs much more in real time. Central Banks can influence the exchange rates, and sometimes actively participate in managing exchange rates. Transactions occur both electronically like equity and over the phone, much like the RFQ process in Fixed Income.

The Derivatives CoP

As described earlier, derivatives are instruments that derive value from other instruments, either equity, fixed income, FX, or commodities. They can be simple like a put or call option, or become very complex, with options on options. There are two main variations of derivatives–listed and *over the counter* (OTC). Listed derivatives, as the naming implies, trade on formal exchanges, like the Chicago Mercantile Exchange (CME) or the Chicago Board Options Exchange (CBOE).

Listed derivatives, as they are based on a formal exchange model, tend to align more with the equity community. Many of the options are based on equities and their trading share price. However, in contrast to the other asset classes, the variations that derivatives introduce create a clear delineation in the expertise and language used within the community. Even in regards to *settlement*—where equity, fixed income, or an asset is exchanged for cash—in the listed derivatives space, many times only cash, after calculating the difference in prices, is exchanged.

OTC gained significant notoriety as the reason for the 2008 global market collapse, due to the underlying risks taken with Credit Default Swaps, among other types of OTC products. Traditionally, OTC products were individual contracts negotiated between two (and sometimes more) firms. These would be lengthy documents with various provisions, and each part uniquely negotiated and different from a similar contract. The International Swaps and Derivatives Association (ISDA) organization is based in London, and looked to simplify and standardize much of this by creation of the *Master Agreement* (ISDA MA or just MA), which handled basic terms across different legal jurisdictions across which firms may be creating the contract.

OTC products have evolved significantly since the 1990s, to the point that they also now are broken down into two further groupings—ones that are more *standardized* and are traded through *Swap Execution Facilities* (SEFs), and those that remain *bilateral* (negotiated directly between two parties).

Further, while derivatives span the other types of asset classes—equity, fixed income, FX and commodities—they do not depend on those communities directly for the majority of processes, procedures, and day to day operations. Much of the language in OTC is more closely related to legal jargon than financial instruments, as they are based on contracts that are enforceable by law in multiple jurisdictions. This also tends to create greater separation from the listed derivatives community.

The Commodity CoP

Commodities are likely the oldest traded asset—based on the original seed markets. The basis of commodities is unlike what equities, fixed income, or FX represents; commodities are assets—typically broken down into metals, energy, livestock/meat, and agricultural. Commodities are often traded using derivatives contracts in order for firms that rely on a specific commodity to budget and manage expenses over time. For example, airlines purchase vast quantities of fuel over time. Through buying a *future*, they can lock in a single price for a long term—six months or a year or more. Otherwise, they would be subject to a rollercoaster of price increases and decreases during that period that could affect their day to day cash flows. Similarly, farmers can sell their harvests ahead of time, at a specific price, protecting themselves from potential drops in price over time.

Many factors affect commodities—most of them unpredictable—from weather to disease to insect infestations to war and natural disasters, making it a highly specialized space. While derivatives are used as a vehicle to reduce risk, much of the focus is around the actual exchange of the physical commodity. There are speculators and those that don't actually need the underlying commodity, but the community only exists because oil, oranges, ox, and ore need to be exchanged in large quantities for basic manufacturing, retail, and livelihood.

CHAPTER 8

The Investment Roadmap

In 2010, a number of the leading standards and industry organizations came together to try and work together in an effort that came to be published as the *Investment Roadmap* (Figure 8.1 and Figure 8.2).[1] The six major organizations (FISD, FIX Protocol Limited, FpML, ISITC, SWIFT, and XBRL US), proposed that the work would be a step toward creating a single business model across the securities business, and enable interoperability. The main goal of the roadmap, from senior sponsors, was to understand where to put investment dollars necessary to shore up and enable some sort of framework focusing on what standards should be used for what processes. There was recognition of the need to find a way to interoperate between established standards that existed in different communities, and across different communities. These, of course, were not the terms used; it was a number of years prior to data becoming a focal point. At the time, regulatory scrutiny was driving requirements that were not possible to implement due to different technology infrastructures, different methodologies and approaches, and different viewpoints across existing silos and business processes.

With the previous chapters on different Communities of Practice within financial services as a basis, now would be a good time to present some of the roadmap—as it provides a very good detailed breakdown of processes within the securities business sector of financial services (our primary concern). The participants recognized some of the complexity that caused friction within the industry, and presented a 2-dimensional model of function and asset class.

---

[1] 2010. "Investment Roadmap." *Fix Trading Community.* https://fixtrading.org/standards/other-standards/investment-roadmap/ (accessed January 4, 2021); 2010. "Progress through Collaboration: A New Investment Roadmap." International Swaps and Derivatives Association. https://isda.org/a/RciDE/press101210.pdf (accessed January 2021).

Investment Roadmap – FIX, ISO, FpML, XBRL syntax (HIGH LEVEL)

	Function	Cash Equities & Fixed Income	Forex[2]	Listed Derivatives	OTC Derivatives[2]	Funds
Issuer	Pre-investment decision		N/A		N/A	
Front Office	Pre-Trade					
Front Office	Trade					
Middle Office	Post-Trade	▲ ○	▲ ○	▲ ○		
Middle Office	Clearing / Pre-Settlement				▲ ○	
Back Office	Asset Servicing	○ ◇	N/A			○ ◇
Back Office	Collateral Management	▲ ○	N/A	▲ ○	□ ○	N/A
Back Office	Settlement					
Back Office	Pricing / Risk / Reporting	□ ○	□ ○	□ ○	□ ○	□ ○
Investor Supervision	Regulatory Reporting	▲ ○	▲ ○	▲ ○		
Issuer Supervision	Regulatory Reporting		N/A		N/A	

▲	FIX	○	ISO (1)
□	FpML	◇	XBRL

(1) Represents ISO 20022, ISO 15022 and MT messages
(2) See OTC Derivatives breakout for details:
- Syndicated Loans, Privately Negotiated FX, and OTC Equity, Interest Rate, Credit, and Commodity Derivatives
- FpML payload may be used in combination with FIX business processes in dealer to buy side communication

Figure 8.1 Roadmap

	Function	Cash Equities & Fixed Income	Forex	Listed Derivatives	OTC Derivatives	Funds
Issuer	**Pre-investment decision:** Filing Fundamental Data with the Regulator, Analytical Models		N/A		N/A	
Front Office	**Pre-Trade:** IOIs, Trade adverts, Quotes, Market data, Short Sale Locate, Reference Data					
Front Office	**Trade:** Order Routing, Trade Execution, Trade Date Position Reporting, Reference Data					
Middle Office	**Post-Trade:** Trade Capture & Validations, Allocation, Matching, Confirmation/Affirmation, Position Management, OTC Derivatives Post Trade Processing					
Middle Office	**Clearing / Pre-Settlement:** Matching, Netting, Funding, Reference Data					
Back Office	**Asset Servicing:** Issuance, Corporate Actions, Proxy Voting, Securities Lending		N/A			
Back Office	**Collateral Management:** Initial Margining, Margin Call, Substitution, Recall, Transfer, Interest Payment		N/A			N/A
Back Office	**Settlement:** Pre-advisement, Settlement Notification, Settlement, Transaction Management, Fail and Claim Management					
Back Office	**Pricing / Risk / Reporting:** Tax Management, Income Collection, Risk Management, Pricing & Valuation, Reporting, Position Management					
Investor Supervision	**Regulatory Reporting:** Short Sale Reporting, Trade Surveillance Reporting, Position Management Reporting, Tax Lot Reporting					
Issuer Supervision	**Regulatory Reporting:** Short Interest Reporting, Financial Statement Reporting, Investment Reporting		N/A		N/A	

Figure 8.2 Roadmap medium level

As a foundation, this gives a nice jumping off point but, as we have seen in previous chapters, it is too simplified for the vastly more complex set of overlapping CoPs that need to be overlayed. Even in this simple two-dimensional model, complexity can be seen in the seemingly *overlapping* standards and solutions in some dimension. However, the presentation hides the reality and seems to infer that the illustrated complexity can be easily solved by picking a single standard when multiple standards intersect.

The effort, given the mix of experts, the various communities they represented, and desire to find *common ground* is a testament to collaborative work within financial services. It is disappointing that it has not been built upon since 2010. However, it is clear that when viewed through the lens of CoPs, it is not a final product and has a number of conflicting inferences. The effort also suffered from the focus seeming to be more a staking of claim by whichever standard dominated a particular defined box. ISITC and FISD were left to mediate conflicts where there was no one clear *winner* for a defined box.

A CoP Analysis of the Roadmap

The Roadmap provides some rudimentary definitions pointing to the existence of CoPs. The first *level* of breakout calls out specific roles that we have previously discussed; issuer, front office, back office, and so forth. The next two *levels* try to capture actual functions that occur within those CoPs; for example, Settlement and Transaction Management as subtasks within *Settlement* that are classified as being a *Back Office* CoP function. On the second dimension, the Roadmap then breaks these across CoPs based on asset type (Equity, Derivatives, and so forth)—with the main differentiation being the type of standard used for that asset type, as well as some level of differentiation where functions are not performed, such as no *preinvestment decision* or *asset servicing* for Forex asset types. These division should sound familiar by now, as we have discussed all of them within the context of different Communities of Practice, as well as how they tend to intersect and overlay each other.

This two dimensional model, however, hides the complexity, and some of the reasoning why multiple standards may be used in some of the intersections, such as FIX and ISO existing in Equity and Fixed Income Post-Trade. It also ignores that while there may be a *singular* standard in a function, it is by no means the universally used standard. It is possible that other methods, not documented in the roadmap, are used—from more manual nonstandards like voice, e-mail, and fax, to standards belonging to other organizations that may not have participated in this specific exercise.

While there appears to be some level of homogeneity for some functions (i.e., ISO being the only standard in *Back Office Settlement*), there is a real argument that this is not consistent across all the CoPs that intersect with that function. For example, in broker-to-broker settlement flows, especially when dealing with global exchanges, firm-specific solutions and FIX are standard.[2] If the Roadmap was contextually bound to only be related to Investment Manager/Buy Side related flows, there may be less variability to contend with. But without beginning with a discipline that includes CoPs first, the roadmap gives a decidedly *flat* view of a much more complex, multidimensional world.

Additionally, applied linguistics (in part) attempts to solve problems of communication *between* communities of practice, which would be better viewed as an interaction diagram. We can imaging our CoP cube (Figure 3.1) rotating, revealing interconnected lines between various, but not all the CoPs. The questions that need to be asked are:

- What is the dominant language spoken by the CoP? Are there other languages of note?
- What is the dominant language spoken by the *target* CoP? Are there other languages?
- What is the language used between the communities, and is it different depending on direction?

---

[2] Is an example; "Nasdaq Clearing provides proprietary tools for accessing the derivatives market. Below you find additional information regarding each of them. Nasdaq Clearing also offers access through OMnet API and FIX, as well as several independent software vendors (ISV)."
NASDAQ Clearing. 2021. "Technology and Connectivity." *NASDAQ clearing technology connectivity for clearing.* https://nasdaq.com/solutions/nasdaq-clearing-technology-connectivity-for-clearing

We may see a little bit of this inferred, such as within Middle Office, Post-Trade, where both FIX and ISO are indicated. This aligns with Front Office—Trade conforming to FIX, and Middle Office—Clearing/Pre-Settlement conforming to ISO. But it is not explicit nor authoritative enough to rely on to make critical decisions regarding communication and standards within and between the CoPs. There are exceptions on different levels, and not always consistently. Asset servicing and Collateral areas have the most obvious diversity, but there is divergence throughout. There is an implied assumption that *standard* and *language* are synonyms. This simplification is wrong, and provides a false foundation that in turn means decisions based on this will also be in error.

And there are additional CoP dimensions not included in this Investment Roadmap model.

- Country and/or regional jurisdiction: These can impact a number of outputs, from language and alphabets used (i.e., Chinese or Japanese, for example), as well as potentially any formal regulation that has mandated certain standards' use such as the Markets in Financial Instruments Directive Part II Regulatory Technical Standard 23 (MiFID II RTS23).
- The demographic of the specific firm: Smaller and mid-market firms may have less investment in any particular technology and be using anything from FAX to CSV over (secure or unsecured) e-mail or SFTP for communication.
- Vertical of observation: As mentioned, the Investment Roadmap was driven much more from the Investment Manager to Broker, with Custodian segment. When observing these flows purely through the Broker—Exchange dynamic, the results would likely be significantly different
- Belies where multiple standards may be in use underneath a *wrapper*, for example, ISO 15022.

CHAPTER 9

Cross Border and Domestic Communities

Is financial services a global activity? As usual, the answer is "it depends." Within a single country, there is a significant amount of trading in the various asset classes, involving the various firm types and actors we have described, using different methods of communication (some of which we explored in the Investment Roadmap), and through the various functional roles. And so, it can be argued that domestic activity plays a substantial role in financial services and can be seen as its own CoP.

In the same way, cross-border activity involves different types of firms, across different countries, with rules that many times conflict. Individuals and firms operating in this space need to be multilingual, not just in human language, but in regulations, processes, customs, and cultures.

The Domestic CoP

Domestic activity involves firms that are based in the same country, trading instruments that are issued and listed in that country, settle through local infrastructures, and are subject to the local rules and regulations. A simple example would be, two firms based in the United States, trading stocks of a United States company, on the NASDAQ Stock Exchange, settled through the Depository Trust and Clearing Company (DTCC). *Domestic* does not always mean "USA." Someone in London would talk about *domestic activity* and be referring to trades settling through CREST and British Pounds (GBP), and in Italy, it would be Monte Titoli in Euros (EUR).

When financial activity is limited to a single jurisdiction, there is a certain assumed simplicity. There are less nuances, and less variation. Infrastructures tend to be more homogeneous and interconnected.

Firms also tend to collapse functions and processes because there is less need for handling a wide array of requirements. In short, operating within a single market is an easily defined Community of Practice. That should not be taken to say that the other CoPs we have already viewed— particularly by asset class and firm type—do not exist. But operating in a single market does provide a foundation of commonality in rules, processes, and expectations.

The Cross Border, or Global, CoP

Cross border, in contrast, refers to activity where at least one aspect of the financial activity is outside the borders of one or more of the firms participating. An Investment Manager in the United States, purchasing shares of BMW, settling through Deutsche Borse in EUR must deal with a number of different factors than would be required by simple U.S. Domestic activity. And interestingly, a German fund manager buying shares in a U.S. Company on the New York Stock Exchange (NYSE) will face similar—but different—processes than the U.S. investor.

In the United States Germany example, we can examine some of the process steps that need to be taken, and the firms involved. Take a U.S. Broker A who has a legal presence in the United States and a German Broker B who has a legal presence in Germany. Due to laws and regulations, as a U.S. entity and under U.S. laws and regulation, the U.S. Broker A has the ability to directly access U.S. Regulated stock exchanges, like the New York Stock Exchange, settle directly at the DTCC, and interact with U.S. registered brokers and investment managers. German Broker B, in order to access U.S. stock exchanges and settle at the DTCC, requires a relationship with a U.S. based broker (US Broker C) who has those same access rights as U.S. Broker A. When German Broker B settles U.S.-based equity or fixed income securities, these still will settle at DTCC, just like U.S. Broker A. However, the instructions that German Broker B provides to their counterparties will be U.S. Broker C's DTCC account information, as well as German Broker B's account information at U.S. Broker C. The settlement, then will actually happen between U.S. Broker A and U.S. Broker C, with U.S. Broker C representing German Broker B.

In a real life example, this simple differentiation could lead to confusion if the non-U.S. operators are not familiar with U.S. domestic operations. In this case, in building a settlement system, the nuance was overlooked. U.S. based operations were told by the non-U.S. (United Kingdom) based firm that they "had their own DTCC account." When asked for the account number, it was not recognized by DTCC. Trades started to fail and pile up, with both sides insisting it was or was not a valid DTCC Participant ID. Effort was made to make parallels, with the globally experienced U.S. staff explaining that they needed the DTCC ID, just like the non-U.S. operators would have a CREST ID in their native United Kingdom. The UK based operators insisted that is what they were providing.

After days of arguing, the UK-based operators finally thought they had the upper hand. They claimed "we know we are right because our settlement agent in the U.S. gave us that number, and told us it was ours" and sent a copy of the e-mail *proof*. As it turned out, the account number was the UK-based firm's account at their U.S. settlement agent. The U.S. settlement agent had not given them the DTCC Participant ID because the non-U.S. operators kept asking them for their account number! Further, the UK-based firm insisted they had a direct DTCC relationship, which directed the flow to a different process reserved for direct DTCC participants.

So on one hand, the knowledge and environment that the domestic CoP operates in requires very specialized and in depth understanding of the local markets. This is contrasted with the wider knowledge of a far broader environment in the Global CoP. This extends to regulations, processes, and the unique language that each CoP must master in order to communicate effectively with their colleagues. A good deal of accommodation and fixing must occur when these two CoPs interact, and if they are not aware of those differences, that will impact their ability to communicate successfully.

Cross Border or Global?

While used interchangeably, these two things can actually have different meanings. Regional financial activity can be cross-border without being truly *global*. And these regional, jurisdictional, activities differ as well. Regionally, activity across the European jurisdictional landscape is cross-border. Although, outside of the United Kingdom and Switzerland, the unification under the Euro has simplified issues. Further, the coordination at the regulatory level has also done away with a number of barriers that impacted understanding and communication. That is not to say they have been removed, but they have been simplified. In contrast, the Asean region hold significantly more diversity, while still being interdependent, economy-wise, as European countries are on each other.

The Asean region has significant diversity in its regulatory frameworks because the many countries have diverse issues they individually face, as well as different cultures that are taken into account. Therefore, when participating the region's financial markets, especially from outside the region, it necessitates specific considerations and knowledge, significantly different than someone who may be familiar with European financial services.

CHAPTER 10

Standards: Background

Standardization enables huge leaps in productivity by taking things or processes that are used by a community repeatedly and in the same way, and ensuring that they are created or applied consistently. Intrinsically, they make sense. Standards in measurement let us do everything from share recipes to build skyscrapers. Without electrical standards, we wouldn't be able to connect power grids across the world. The same stands for telecommunications and communicating with someone halfway across the globe. Our goal in this chapter is to give a background on standards and why they are important. The next chapter will explore standards within financial services.

Standards have history, starting back centuries when informal standards for everyday life emerged. Early examples include measuring distance by paces (Greek origin, accounting for two steps, approximately two and one half to three feet), cubit (India origin, length of the forearm from elbow to the tip of the middle finger), or a span (length of an outstretched hand). Some of these became formalized, such as the weight measurement *stone*, previously somewhat variable due to the use of actual stones, which is now *officially* 6.35 kilograms, or 14 pounds, and an inch, formerly the width of an adult male thumb. And this led to establishment of formal standards organizations in the 1800s, which we will discuss in a bit more detail later. From all these examples, it should be apparent that consistency in certain shared interests has a wider benefit to the community. Standards enable a foundation for other activities—building roads, selling goods, and communicating.

The introduction of standards would seem to bring with it answers, simplicity, and certainty. And this is a commonly held view that influences legislation, regulators, decisions that firms make in investments, and down to the basic levels of how development and operations are crafted. What should already be coming into question, however, is how different

Communities of Practice would be able to standardize around single solutions, especially given the different languages spoken, not to mention processes, culture, purpose, and needs. Are standards, and the way they are approached within financial services helping, hurting, or a source of confusion? Do standards represent a single simple solution for all, the proverbial *silver bullet*? Or do we need to recognize that silver bullets only work for a specific community—that is, they only kill werewolves—and other solutions and standards are needed for different communities. Because silver bullets do not kill vampires. And the wooden stakes that kill vampires do nothing against werewolves.

Short History of Standards Organizations

The International Telecommunications Union, founded 1865, and Rhine Navigation Commission, founded 1815, are generally held as the two oldest standards organizations. ITU enabled the interoperability of the early telegraph systems. The mechanization that characterized the Industrial Revolution led to the first early standards (in screw thread sizes), innovations such as the interchangeable part, and establishment of the Engineering Standards Committee in 1901. The International Organization for Standardization (ISO) was established in 1947, as a replacement for the suspended ISA (in 1942, due to WWII), which had an original mission to enhance international cooperation for standards.

The naming of these standards organizations belie the fact that there are hundreds, if not thousands, of other standards organizations across the world, including national bodies, industry specific organizations, and international organizations focused on a sector or specific purpose (such as W3C—the World Wide Web Consortium). Following from this diversity of organizations, there are a multitude more actual standards, so that trying to identify them all would be an exercise without end—as keeping the list updated with changes, additions, and deprecations would likely be more than a full time job.

To even talk about standards, we already have to start putting them in boxes. Looking functionally at something seemingly innocuous like *messaging* and there arises a need to immediately qualify. First, we should pull away purely technological standards—like "XML" (as opposed to XBRL), or specific programming languages, API methodologies, or things like SFTP, e-mail, cloud-based document share drives, and the like. The reasoning here is that these are not *financial industry* specific; they are tools that are used to perform various functions and build solutions, but don't represent financial-specific instances.[1]

The word *standard* also conveys certain things, and lends the label to infer more than intended, and create a bias because of this assigned label or certification. Much of this comes down to commercial concerns, marketing, and narrative. And, in the end, solving for a specific CoP. An excellent example of this is the history between the VHS and Betamax standards.

"The notion of language standards is closely tied to the notion of public or private 'authorities' that set and seek to maintain those standards, however arbitrary, and far from the 'linguistic facts' that they may be. Such efforts are typically not really about language at all, but about establishing or protecting the power of a group through the language or variety they speak."[2] This should be kept in mind as we explore standards in financial services as follows.

Betamax vs VHS

Sony launched Betamax in 1975, a full year ahead of the JVC launch of VHS. Betamax, in general opinion, had a higher quality and technical superiority. It is accepted that Betamax had superior sound and video, and that the corresponding machines for recording and playback were of a higher quality.

In contrast, VHS had a lower quality, but allowed for a longer recording time per tape, at 120 minutes, almost double that of Betamax. On average, VHS had a lower cost per playback and recording machine. For the consumer, then, they had to weigh the benefits of a better picture against the inconvenience of changing out tapes in the middle of a feature-length movie, and if that was worth the increased price.

---

[1] Again, from the bias of the CoP of the author. Some may rightly argue that any of these are financial services standards from their own CoP perspective.

[2] Hall, Smith, Wicaksono. 2011. *Mapping Applied Linguistic*, 27. New York, NY: Routledge.

In the end, VHS was able to capture a majority of the market share, despite its later launch, marketing on convenience, price, and wider availability (JVC would license VHS technology to many manufacturers while Sony held the Betamax standard technology close). Sony tried to appeal to the Japanese Ministry of Trade and Industry, claiming VHS infringement on Betamax. While Betamax would eventually create versions that matched the length of VHS, it continued to emphasize quality over affordability. The community interested in paying more for the relative quality difference would prove be a minority.

Both of these were valid standards, however, and served different communities. Further, during this time, other tape video standards were introduced (such as Video2000 and Laserdiscs from Philips or Catrivision from Sanyo) that helped drive the further evolution of both Betamax and VHS. Despite this, Betamax and VHS remained the two video standards that existed until the advent of the CD and DVD technologies.

When a Standard Is Not Standard

As we talk about standards, and the proliferation of international standards bodies, national standards bodies, and industry specific standards bodies, the thought goes to ask if all those organizations agree what is a standard. While, in spirit, there is a general feeling that "a standard is a standard," how it is described, and the nuances that surround different definitions begin to paint a more opaque picture.

The European Committee for Standardization (CEN) defines a standard as:

A standard (French: Norme, German: Norm) is a technical document designed to be used as a rule, guideline or definition. It is a consensus-built, repeatable way of doing something. Standards are created by bringing together all interested parties such as manufacturers, consumers and regulators of a particular material, product, process or service. All parties benefit from standardization through increased product safety and quality as well as lower transaction costs and prices.[3]

Meanwhile, the British Standards Institute (BSI) defines it thusly:

> [I]n essence, a standard is an agreed way of doing something. It could be about making a product, managing a process, delivering a service or supplying materials—standards can cover a huge range of activities undertaken by organizations and used by their customers.
>
> Standards are the distilled wisdom of people with expertise in their subject matter and who know the needs of the organizations they represent—people such as manufacturers, sellers, buyers, customers, trade associations, users or regulators.
>
> Our portfolio extends to more than 30,000 current standards. They are designed for voluntary use, so it's up to you—you're not forced to follow a set of rules that make life harder for you; you're offered ways to do your work better.
>
> Standards are knowledge. They are powerful tools that can help drive innovation and increase productivity. They can make organizations more successful and people's everyday lives easier, safer and healthier.[4]

So, then, even within standards, there is a lack of a single agreed view of what a standard is, how it is defined, who should use them, and who is the authority. This becomes extremely important when decisions are made based on certain standards or standards setting organization (SSO). There are commercial impacts, competitive and anti-competitive

---

[3] European Committee for Standardization. 2021. "What is a Standard?" *European Committee for Standardization, Standards Development.* https://cen.eu/work/ENdev/whatisEN/Pages/default.aspx (accessed January 4, 2021).

[4] BSI. 2021. "What is a Standard?" *Understand Standards and Schemes for Certification, Information about Standards.* https://bsigroup.com/en-US/Standards/Information-about-standards/What-is-a-standard/ (accessed January 4, 2021).

concerns, potential for creation of unintended monopolies through regulatory mandates, and real costs that can work against the intent of why standards exist, and why standards are important.

Further, there is a disagreement on if something that purports to be a standard but is not officially recognized by a formal standards organization is actually a standard. Herein lays some of the politics of linguistics, and a variation on our linguistic theme of 'right' or 'wrong' language. Taking the spirit of what a standard is meant to convey, especially from the BSI definition, it should follow that if something 'standard' satisfies a need of a specific CoP, it should be not be *looked down upon* as unworthy because it does not have the codified blessing of some organized standards body. The *consensus agreement* has effectively been reached within the CoP. There are issues of maintenance and some formal process for maintaining it, but it would seem presumptuous of those outside of the CoP to tell that community that its solution does not meet the standard of being a standard.

In much the same way, terms like *proprietary* are used to describe *standards* that are created by single institutions and then shopped for adoption by the larger community. Again, language plays a role here as the inference is that *proprietary* somehow means *lesser* and conveys that the *owner* is seeking to leverage some kind of competitive advantage. Indeed, this can be the case in many instances, as companies like Apple have created a *standard* environment for their products that introduces barriers for competition and from user change. However, as we will see with efforts like the Financial Product Markup Language (FpML), there are just as many instances where a large corporation looks to solve a community problem, and subsequently, hands that solution over to the community.

As we quoted previously from Hall, Smith, and Wicaksono, many times, the posturing or assertion by standards organizations over solutions that are not under their umbrella is more about power, and maintaining control, and many times at the cost and negative impact to the communities in need.

CHAPTER 11

Standards in 2020 Financial Services

Birth of Financial Services Standards: Identifiers, Messaging Protocols

Financial services standards have played a critical role in the modern environment. A well-worn story that is typically used as an example is the paper crunch on Wall Street. By 1968, the firms that comprised the whole of the securities business had reached a tipping point. Everything up to that point was based in paper and individual transactions done by hand. An average of 6 million shares traded daily by the end of 1965, growing to 13 million by 1968. On June 13, 1968, 21 million shares were traded, beating the previous single-day record of 16 million set on October 29, 1929.

Famously, firms—including the New York Stock Exchange—had to close every Wednesday to clear backlog. Further, millions of certificates would be lost or stolen. As discussed, this led to the creation of the pre-cursor of the Depository Trust Corporation, the first modern Central Securities Depository, and the CUSIP (Committee on Uniform Security Identification Procedures) identifier. This enabled the slow elimination of the physical exchange of millions of certificates a day, allowing volumes to increase without needing to shut down the industry every Wednesday.

As stated previously, while serving the needs of a specific community, standards can have significant positive effect not just for that group, but also on society as a whole. But the establishment of standards also needs to be weighed against the potential for improper commercial exploitation, possible barriers to change and the cost implications associated with revising an existing standard versus adopting something new. There can be significant money involved in standards—JVS's VHS standard would collect significant royalties from those to whom it licensed the technology, above and beyond what products itself sold directly.

As trade volume and activity increase, and as the speed of information becomes more important, standards are looked to provide those incremental boosts of efficiency. There is only so much manual hands are able to do, and there is a diminishing rate of return of throwing bodies at a problem. As technology increasing takes center stage for increasing volumes, velocity of data, and the ability to consume the variety of data, and maintain its veracity (the four "V"s of data management), standards become critical as tools to enable consistent communication among market participants.

At the same time, globalization continues to accelerate, introducing more complexity in the form of jurisdictional CoP based regulation, process and procedures, language, and format differences across language barriers and CoP barriers, and forcing the need for better cross-CoP understanding and multilingualism.

Given this, we should examine the organizations that create and maintain standards within financial services. First, there is no global standards-setting authority and no federation that coordinates all the various standards efforts. In the majority of cases, participants are volunteers with their time and effort effectively donated by individual firms for the greater good. But, as noted in the previous chapter, there are many standards organizations vying for the singular authority in this space, mostly in an effort to maintain control and power in regards to their view of how things should be done.

In the following Figure 11.1, the goal is to map the high level standards that are relevant in the area of financial services we are discussing. This is by no means a complete picture. Former Commissioner of the SEC, Dan Gallagher created a "Crazy Quilt Chart of Regulation," which paints a similar overwhelming picture of the regulations that are imposed on US financial firms.[1] The goal of both are to help illustrate the complexity, and

---

[1] SEC Commissioner Daniel M. Gallagher. "Rules Applicable to U.S. Financial Services Holding Company Adopted Since July 2010." *Financial Services Holding Company Rules.* https://sec.gov/news/speech/2015/financial-services-holding-companies-rules-2.pdf, (accessed January 4, 2021).

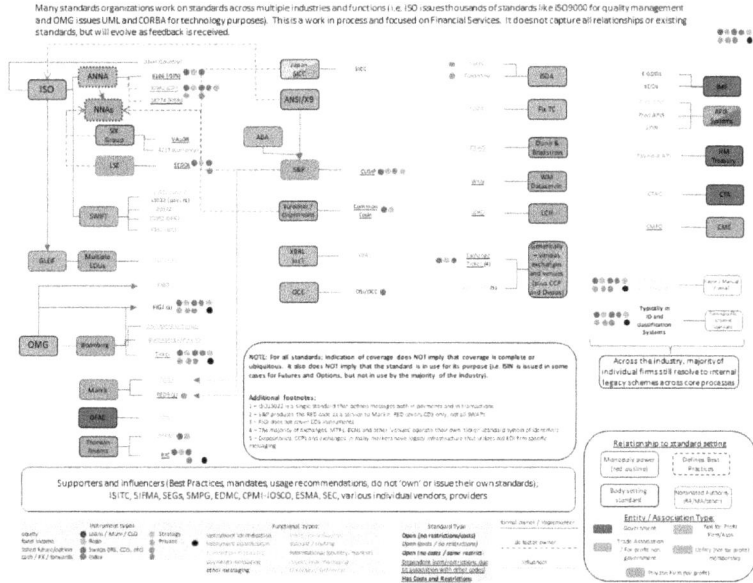

Figure 11.1 Standards graph

interconnectedness, of the different standards (in my case) or regulations (per Mr. Gallagher), as well as the variety of standards.

Looking at the organizations that create and promote these standards, it should be noted that they also have a wide variety of structures, cultures, and forms. Some tend to serve specific communities (such as ISDA for Swaps and Derivatives), while others look to be everything for everyone (such as ISO), providing more of a *library* function, without paying much attention to the diversity of communities—or more often the lack thereof—participating and being affected by those standards.

Additionally, there are organizations that view and incorporate existing standards and create *best practices* for implementing or using those standards for their specific communities (ISITC fits into this category), and sometimes also create their own standards in parallel (such as the FIX organization). Some organizations actively lobby to promote their standards in regulation, policy, and law while others expressly avoid doing so, seeing it as a conflict of interests. And some organizations exist primarily to lobby on behalf of their community. This all leads to significant confusion and opportunity for misunderstandings, misrepresentations, and unintended consequences. Especially if an adopter or regulator is uninformed of the true scope, or lack thereof, of a standard or organization promoting it, the wrong assumptions may be made about applicability for a specific community (or trying to apply a specific community's solution to a wider group).

No single model solves for all problems. I provided the allegory of the silver bullet only killing werewolves, not vampires. Understanding the organizations involved, the representation allowed (or not allowed) and the kind of expertise each group has is critical for the industry, users, and regulators to determine where to address certain problems or approaches for particular information or expertise.

Much like standards themselves, there are communities that support different organizations, each with different membership models and focuses. While *de facto* standards exist outside of formal standards organizations, implementation models vary. There is also a level of commercial interest by some participants, which has an impact on promotion (lobbying/mandates), use (or restrictions), and functionality (or lack thereof) of some *standards*.

The Various Standards Bodies

I apologize to the many organizations not included in this discussion. Some I may have missed given that they operate on the edges of the primary subject matter of this book (e.g., Financial Services), or I am not familiar enough with them to properly include them. However, I will clearly state that I have not included or gone into any serious depth regarding standards organizations that, while they have a decided interest in Financial Services, that is not their primary focus. This includes the many technology standards groups surrounding operating system platforms (Linux Foundation, Unbuntu, etc.), programming (Jupyter, others) and organizations like Mozilla, the World Wide Web Consortium (W3C), Institute of Electrical and Electronics Engineers (IEEE), and so on. The table (Table A.1) referenced at the end of this book summarizes many of the organizations, and highlights organization and operation. But it will be helpful to indicate some of the primary players that have a larger influence in conversations relevant to our topic.

Many of these organizations came into being through the sheer will of an individual or group that faced a shared problem. Many starting as humble beginnings—two or three people around a coffee table or at a bar trying to resolve a particular problem or issue. Fast forward five or ten years, and hundreds of people are converging onto a conference location.

In the previous chapter, I allude to some of the benefits standards bring to the industries or communities for which they are created. I ask, however, what qualifies an organization to be a creator of any standard, what policies apply, how is the process supported, and what are the risks—even in light of the benefits? There are *formal* standards organizations—some of them already mentioned earlier—and there are organizations that due to their position in the marketplace, or subject matter expertise, end up being *de facto* standards creators. Some of this gets couched in language such as *proprietary* and *nonproprietary*, which introduces its own nuances and issues.

Formal standards organizations have a variety of different participation structures, membership, and funding models. A few unifying themes and beliefs persist among these organizations:

- Standards help create innovation
- Standards should help create competition
- Standards development should avoid anti-competitive/anti-trust issues
- Focus should be on creating well-formed standards

Table A.1 in the Appendix summarizes a good number of these different organizations that were also referenced in Figure 11.1. To illustrate the aforementioned four goals, I will reference some of these organizations' mission statements.

ASC X9

The Accredited[2] Standards Committee X9 (ASC X9) in support of the financial services industry has the mission to create and maintain U.S. and International standards that improve payments and securities transactions, protect data and facilitate information exchange.

ASC X9 fulfills the objectives of:
- Support (maintain, enhance, and promote use of) existing standards

---

[2] Accredited by the American National Standard Institute (ANSI)

- Facilitate development of new, open standards based upon consensus
- Provide a common source for all standards affecting the Financial Services Industry
- Focus on current and future standards needs of the Financial Services Industry
- Promote use of Financial Services Industry standards
- Participate and promote the development of international standards[3]

ISO

ISO's "strategic vision for 2016-2020" is,

> ISO will Develop high-quality standards through ISO's global membership, by ensuring we effectively Engage stakeholders and partners. A strong foundation in People and organization development, effective Use of technology, and a focus on Communication, will help us to achieve the ultimate objective of ISO standards used everywhere.[4]

OMG

The mission of the Object Management Group (OMG) is to develop technology standards that provide real-world value for thousands of vertical industries. OMG is dedicated to bringing together its international membership of end-users, vendors, government agencies, universities, and research institutions to develop and revise these standards as technologies change throughout the years.[5]

W3C

The W3C mission is to lead the World Wide Web to its full potential by developing protocols and guidelines that ensure the long-term growth of

---

[3] Accredited standards committee X9. January 4, 2021. "Mission and Objectives." https://x9.org/missions-and-objectives/ (accessed January 4, 2021).

[4] ISO. 2015. January 4, 2021. "ISO Strategy 2016-2020," https://iso.org/files/live/sites/isoorg/files/store/en/PUB100364.pdf (accessed January 4, 2021).

[5] OMG. 2021. "Mission statement." *Object Management Group.* https://omg.org/about/index.htm, (accessed January 4, 2021).

the Web. This is based on "Web For All" and "Web on Everything" design principles and vision for the Web [that] involves participation, sharing knowledge, and thereby building trust on a global scale.[6]

British Standards Institute

BSI is a world-leading national standards body that helps our clients operate in a way that is safer, more secure and more sustainable. Incorporated by Royal Charter, we're truly impartial, and home to the ultimate mark of trust, the Kitemark.

Our unique combination of consulting, knowledge, assurance and regulatory services makes organizations more resilient, and in turn inspires trust in their products, systems, services, and the world we live in.

Our purpose

Inspiring trust for a more resilient world.

Our mission

To share knowledge, innovation and best practice to help people and organizations make excellence a habit.

Our vision

To be the business improvement company that enables organizations to turn standards of best practice into habits of excellence.[7]

FIX

FIX Trading Community is built around clear standards

FIX Protocol is part of the fabric of capital markets. Formed in 1991 at the dawn of electronic trading, FIX connects the global ecosystem of venues, asset managers, banks/brokers, vendors and regulators by standardizing the communication among participants. This is accomplished by following four key principles:

1. Creating and maintaining robust open standards across the whole ecosystem from pretrade to market data to settlement.
2. Providing advice and counsel to regulatory bodies in a transparent and unbiased way.

---

[6] World wide web consortium. 2021. "W3C Mission." https:// w3.org/Consortium/ mission (accessed January 4, 2021).

[7] BSI. 2021. "Our purpose, Mission, and Vision." https://bsigroup.com/en-US/ about-bsi/inspiring-trust-for-a-more-resilient-world/ (accessed January 4, 2021).

3. Seeking ways to improve the trading process front to back for the global financial services industry.

4. Providing our members with a neutral, collaborative environment to come together through member-driven conferences and other critical forums to promote, support and educate.[8]

Within each of these statements belies some perspectives regarding their focus on community and applicability of their standards. In most cases, the statements are broad, although nonexclusionary. The exception would be ISO, which would seem to state that it is only "ISO standards that are used everywhere." ANSI/X9 specifically states its scope toward Financial Services, and within payments and securities. W3C's focus is purely on accessibility to the World Wide Web. BSI and OMG both aim toward improvement, while OMG specifically notes the nature of change over time. FIX, like OMG, clearly states its support for open standards and collaboration. To support these aims, organizations use many different models, which have different impacts. They end up having a connecting theme to our previous deep dive into the different ways to view the financial services industry, and the different perspectives under which those communities operate.

ISO: International Organization for Standardization

It would be wrong to point to one group and say, "That is the right way to do standards" or "That is the wrong way to do standards."[9] On one hand, the International Organization for Standardization (ISO) has a long history of issuing global standards with meaningful and far-reaching implications. On the other hand, an organization like the Financial Information eXchange (FIX) was created to address the specific needs of front office communications about pretrade and trade details for a specific community. A big difference here is that in many cases, it is not ISO or its Technical Committees that have actually developed or created

---

[8] FIX trading community. January 4, 2021. "Mission Statement." https://fixtrading.org/mission-statement/ (accessed January 4, 2021).

[9] I refer back to there being no *right* or *wrong* language

standards it issues. In these cases, other standardization organizations create community-focused standards, and after a period of time, bring those to ISO as a formality for registration and receipt of the *ISO brand*. This has started to change in recent years, which brings with it some bigger issues regarding applicability of these ISO standards to different CoPs that are not effectively represented at ISO (nor likely to be).

ISO provides a needed function of bringing together multiple national and pan-national standards organizations and regimes, which we will see is itself a specific and limited community. Where there is a specific use-case that can be applied consistently, an ISO process can make sense. ISO also adopts standards created by designated *liaison* organizations when they align with a similar ISO standard or fall into an interest area of a working group. However, ISO membership is restricted to limited and nominated participation. While this ensures democratic and equal numerical representation for each country member, it does introduce practical issues when addressing specific, bespoke, or localized needs.

There is also the concern of actual domain expertise. When participants at ISO are members of a national standards organization, they likely are either generalists, or have expertise in a specific area. In either case, this naturally limits any ability to deep-dive into the majority of standards brought before them, and these individual representatives are therefore left to rely on their own references (their own community), which may or may not have any practical overlap with the community the proposed standard is meant for. Also, ISO itself is not a specific financial services standards organization, but has over 100 different *Technical Committees*, only one of which is for financial services.

Object Management Group

In contrast to ISO, an organization like the Object Management Group has multiple tiers of membership, based partially on firm type, revenue, and size, as well as allowing individuals, with varying levels of access and voting rights. OMG is a liaison into some ISO Technical Committees, and is allowed to participate in discussions and standards development, and comment, but not vote.

OMG participants tend to be very technical, coming from software engineering, computer science, and similar backgrounds due to the core nature of OMG's work. As such, as a community, even in the financial services space, participants tend to be less from the *business side* of the world, and much more focused on the technical and data problems formally. Indeed, as of September 2020, there is a key working group, titled "Vocabulary for Community of Interest (COI)" with an assembled group of experts in ontology, system engineering, linguistics, and semantics that are decomposing the problem of data in context, across community. Full disclosure, I am part of this group, and introduced the expanded scope of Community beyond the context and ontology concepts. But, again, this group has much less direct knowledge of actual expertise performing the various financial services functions. But the group does try to stay self-aware of that, and is merely proposing creation of a methodology, as opposed to an implementation and solution to the problem.

FIX

FIX began as a discussion among the front offices of Fidelity and Salomon Brothers to find a way to reduce or eliminate the communication of trades and trading information over the telephone. For every trade or transaction, one side had to call the other and exchange information verbally, and then enter this information in their respective computer systems.

Interestingly, FIX began its life at much the same time, around the late 1980s and early 1990s that SWIFT had brought the work that would be the ISO 7775 standard into ISO. While SWIFT's CoP focused around custodian banks and payments, the FIX CoP was much more fast paced, and composed of the dynamics of the front office. FIX's approaches have been more informal through the years, in contrast to the more traditional world of ISO. But again, this fit the needs and expectations of the FIX Community and need to respond to changes quickly to incorporate changes in its messaging protocol.

International Swaps Dealer Association (ISDA)

ISDA, formed in 1985, serves the community of swaps dealers and derivatives practitioners. A highly complex environment, derivatives originally were very customized, and each deal resulted in a unique *instrument* or contract. In an effort to reduce risk, ISDA's primary work was in creating a standard Master Agreement that all derivatives contracts could be based on, with consistent legal language. This extended to Credit Support Annexes, and working groups focused on various aspects of the OTC trade flow.

In 1997 to 1999, JPMorgan and PriceWaterhouseCoopers published the first messaging standard specifically for derivatives utilizing the new XML standard, the Financial Product Markup Language (FpML), and the open source FpML organization to manage the standard. In 2001, ISDA agreed to integrate this into their organizational structure.[10]

eXtensible Business Reporting Language (XBRL)

Also based on the XML standard, xBRL began in the late 1990s, and eventually reached version v2.1 that was considered the first official *stable version*, published in 2003. xBRL is a global framework for exchanging business information, typically around accounting and regulatory reporting, although not limited to those areas.[11]

Other Organizations

Organizations such as the W3C (XML, HTML, CSS), DublinCore Metadata Initiative, FIX Organization (FIXML), ISDA (FpML), and Object Management Group (FIGI, FIBO, CORBA) are examples of global standards bodies that have more open membership policies than ISO, and more focused subject matter agendas. This allows more firms to participate (and in some cases, individuals), as well as a more tailored community-focus such that the right expertise is being tapped. These structures are more appropriate for their constituents and functions than going through an organization like ISO.

This kind of membership structure encourages greater participation from interested parties (ISO allows liaison organizations, but they must go

---

[10] FpML. 2021. "History of FpML," https://fpml.org/about/history/ (accessed January 4, 2021).
[11] xBRL. 2021. "The Business Reporting Standard." https://xbrl.org/ (accessed January 4, 2021).

through a vetting process and do not always have equal representation). Open membership prevents domination by one or a few specific sectors through wider participation. It also tends to have more of a larger community-specific population and a variety of subject matter experts involved in the process. This model can produce better, faster results when problems are less homogenous, are highly variable and need greater flexibility.

Two related types of organizations also deserve mention. Independent organizations and individual firms that provide specific services commonly end up creating *de facto*, or *proprietary* standards. In financial instrument identification (i.e., equities, fixed income, and so forth), code standards like RIC (Reuters Identification Code), SEDOL (Stock Exchange Daily Official List), and RED (Reference Entity Data) are all *de facto* standards used in specific processes based on trade lifecycle, jurisdiction, or asset type. Support firms and organizations also play a key role in support of standards. Registration Authorities, such as Bloomberg (FIGI for OMG) or SWIFT (15022, 20022, 9362, 13616, 10383 for ISO), administer the standard and provide support services while organizations like ISITC create Best Practices across the industry. Others, such as FIX (FIXML) or ISDA (FpML), do this in-house or as part of an associated foundation.

Understanding these organizations and their expertise is critical for the industry as it helps users and regulators determine how to solve problems. Existence of one standard does not invalidate the use or need for a similar existing standard from another organization. Use case and target community is more important than the sponsoring standards organization. More effort needs to be made to interoperate and coordinate between organizations and their particular *standard* versus competing to be the *one standard that rules them all*. Recognition that one standard or organization should not be elevated above one or another is something that is both currently lacking and negatively impacts the industry.

Standards—Organization Structures and Purpose

Membership and Impact on Standards

Alluded to during the introduction to standards, there is an aspect of membership and involvement in standards. There are a number of pieces to this, from the policies of involvement to the sociological reasons for participating by both the standards organization and the individuals and firms that become involved. These feed back to our core concept of communities, and influence the aspects of control that are exercised through language policies and standards activities. A primary question the reader should be ready to ask now is: What Community of Practice does any particular standards organization serve, and does its community reflect the CoPs it will impact with its standards, and the active promotion of those standards?

Membership methodologies fall into two broad categories; either open access or some sort of membership qualification. In many standards organizations, there is some level of qualification required to participate. On one level, this makes sense. It is an attempt to align the defined scope of activities with the relevant community, and keep focus. Or it is an attempt to create a more balanced representation of stakeholders so that one group cannot *stack* membership and voting in its favor. This can backfire, however, when trying to create more equality among one community axis results in dominance by a different community. Further, many of these are *invite only* organizations, or are subject to an application where the incumbents can refuse admission. Finally, there can be an aspect of *pay to play* where, even if one meets the membership criteria, there is a required fee to be paid for the privilege of participation.

Membership Example: ISO and National Standard Bodies

There are some formal structures that exist, and formal relationships between different organizations. One of the largest inter-related standards infrastructure comprises national standards bodies (NSB's) and the International Organization for Standardization (ISO). Almost every country in the world has an organization that has been identified as that nation's primary standards body. This may be formal through governmental recognition, or just a de facto basis.

These NSB's focus on standards specific to their national, domestic needs. While many of these needs do spill over to international concerns, the bias is toward national issues and needs, across industries. These NSB's then can become members of ISO, and participate at ISO in the interests of their sponsoring NSB and as a proxy for their national interest.

For example, ANSI/X9 is the Financial Services division of the U.S. national standards organization, the Accredited National Standards Institute. Membership to X9 is open to any firm, with a preferred focus in financial services. There are five levels of membership, which impact voting, level of participation, and access to resources, such as no-fee or discounted fee access to X9 standards.

ISO membership is determined by National Standards Body status. Only those bodies determined to be the *National Standards Body* of a country may belong to ISO, and have voting privileges, much like the United Nations. Other nonprofit industry organizations and government bodies may petition to be liaison members and participate in group discussions and debates, but cannot vote on standards. For-profit firms that are determined to have a unique position in the marketplace may apply to be liaisons as well. So, in order to participate and vote in ISO, any firm or individual will typically need to first belong to their national body (i.e., ANSI/X9), with one of the top-tier memberships, and be nominated to represent the interests of their country's standards group (and not the company they represent at their country level.).

However, participants in NSB's that then go on to also participate in ISO typically come from a pool that lacks diversity. Even for standards intended to impact the entirety of the financial services community as a whole, those that craft those standards come from a small, homogenous group that excludes the representation of the vast majority of even the few Communities of Practice already discussed. Further, the global inclusion ignores where there may be a shared collective—such as the European Union—that has a singular regulatory and governmental jurisdiction, yet still can represent within ISO as individual countries (and vote individually, easily overwhelming nonunified countries). And while there is diverse global representation, the majority come from large industry infrastructure communities for equity settlement, and do not include any expertise from brokers, investment managers, front office, middle office, fixed income, commodities, and so forth.[12]

This is not necessarily intentional. In many cases, there is a lack of available subject matter expertise in a particular subject, but still a need.

---

[12] "SWIFT: Cooperative Governance for Network Innovation, Standards and Community" by Susan V. Scott and Marcos Zachariadis.

This can be because there are very few experts worldwide, and they are busy with other work, there is no connection to the CoP of experts, or there is some other bias at work. The desire to address the issue typically over-rules the lack of that expertise availability. As noted in our discussion on expertise, capable, intelligent professionals will easily be swayed that their expertise can be leveraged for something outside of their area. Further, there is a misapplication of CoP due to bias. Standards practitioners belong to the esoteric and small Standards Community of Practice. Therefore, anything that is a *standard* is seen as within their wheelhouse and fair game, even if the actual CoP it is meant for is not included or participating in any way.

In an *open access* model, membership is open to anyone who wishes to join. They do not need to meet some particular profile. While this should encourage broader participation, it may dilute the focus on more community-specific needs or introduce noise into an effort by partici-pants that have unrelated needs to a particular program. To further com-plicate matters, just because an organization is *closed* does not mean that the standards it produces are *closed*, nor does an *open access* organization necessarily mean that the standards they produce are *open*.

Funding, even in open access organizations presents a challenge, as even volunteer organizations need some level of capital to function. There still is the presence of a *pay to play* model, which can give more power and influence to organizations with deeper pockets, through benefits such as enhanced voting rights or board memberships that steer the focus of any efforts.

In both types (closed and open), standards are either freely available to the world, only available to the community belonging (through some form of membership payment or criteria) to the organization, or only available for a fee. In both models, there are some that fund their activities through methods other than membership fees, such as staging events to raise working capital—from extravagant conferences (though many times very simple events) to simple networking get-togethers at a bar, and col-lecting a cover charge.

However, apart from these activities, some organizations use the stan-dards themselves as a funding mechanism. An organization like ISO which is closed—yet does not have a *pay to play* model—licenses the majority of the standards under the ISO banner, and the Registration Authorities and Maintenance Agencies that manage those standards are also able to extract fees. Meanwhile, the Object Management Group allows anyone to join, under a paid membership model, yet all output is open and free as a public good.

Why Get Involved?

So, why would an organization or individual become involved in any of these organizations? And in doing so, why choose one over another? As previously referenced, standards work, especially regarding established standards, can become primarily about protecting the power of those in control and using those standards. And, as with the VCR, standards can be quite lucrative. Interestingly, when new methodologies, or languages, are proposed, there is backlash. Indeed, you see "…workplace language policies promoting one language" [the incumbent] "over others" which "are essentially attempts to gain or maintain power and control over individuals and groups who are perceived as threatening and whose language or variety are thus a target for public criticism and even legislation."[13]

That is not to say that is the intent of all who work in standards. Far from it. The goals of organizations, from ISO to W3C to OMG to FIX to NSBs like ANSI/X9 and BSI/IST12, all are based in promoting standards for the good of the community, as noted earlier. And firms and individuals join those organizations to support and advance those goals. Some, however, participate expressly to maintain dominance or power, or protect a franchise. The introduction of PVC pipes into the iron pipe world is a clear example of the actions various standards owners will take in protecting their franchise. Both the PVC industry[14] and the iron pipe industry[15] publicly and privately battle regarding their individual standards' benefits over the other.

---

[13] Hall, Smith, Wicaksono. 2011. *Mapping Applied Linguistic*, 27. New York, NY: Routledge.

[14] The Vinyl Institute. 2018. "Two-Faced Claims by the Iron Pipe Industry." https://vinylverified.com/blog/2018/8/29/two-faced-claims-by-the-iron-pipe-industry, (accessed July 2020).

[15] Hanson, R.H., 2016. Letter to City of Burton, MI. https://static1.squarespace.com/static/56748c1d25981d39eaa27bed/t/5a3157b853450a1a416f8478/1513183160422/DIPRA+letter+to+Mayor+Zelenko.pdf (accessed July 2020).

The case of Microsoft Office Open XML presents the accusation that Microsoft used its global presence in pursuit of ISO standardization. Richard Stallman, head of the Free Software Foundations stated

> Microsoft corrupted many members of ISO in order to win approval for its phony 'open' document format, OOXML. This was so governments that keep their documents in a Microsoft-only format can pretend that they are using 'open standards.' The government of South Africa has filed an appeal against the decision, citing the irregularities in the process.[16]

This included placing Microsoft employees as representatives in individual National Bodies and then as ISO representatives across the world, effectively meaning that the *diverse* country group voting were all still a single community of Microsoft employees.[17]

This kind of behavior in ISO and other standards efforts, and similar kinds of abuse are sometimes difficult to find, and cases are not transparently analyzed. Not only is ISO loathe to take action, but has actively worked to prevent any public knowledge.[18] Accusations of dominance persist across ISO Technical Committees, as well as within some other industry and standards organizations. The author should disclose that he has leveled such accusations against ISO in the financial services sector, specifically around a global trade organization composed of individual country monopolies that manages to stack its members much in the way Microsoft had done.

Nor is this limited to single firms or cooperatives with aligned interests. Countries, as noted with the European Union block, also are able to exert a form of dominance in these kinds of forums, and participate

---

[16] Dr. Schestowitz, R. 2008. "ISO and Microsoft: The Corruption Resumes" http://techrights.org/2008/07/11/ooxml-corruption-resumes/ (accessed July 2020).

[17] Dr. Schestowitz, R. 2009. "Company that Attacks ODF Gains More Control of ODF (and why Open Source Should be Careful, Too)." http://techrights.org/2009/10/02/odf-tc-hijack/ (accessed July 2020).

[18] Dr. Schestowitz, R. 2009. "ISO Urged to Invalidate OOXML as Microsoft's Role Gets Shown; More Smears of ODF Come from Microsoft." http://techrights.org/2009/10/17/iso-allies-bashing-odf/ (accessed July 2020),

both to advance their goals and prevent competition from individual or smaller interest groups, even if those solutions are appropriate.
Allowing their acceptance or endorsement in ISO would provide equal
footing for competition. This behavior is not limited to ISO, however,
I should stress that fact.

Outside of ISO, such an example occurred in 1988, in Allied Tube v
Indian Head Inc.[19]

> Fearing that PVC would cut into their market, defendant Allied
> Tube and Conduit Corporation and other steel conduit makers
> collectively agreed to 'pack' the 1980 NFPA meeting with new
> NFPA members, whose only function would be to vote against
> Indian Head's PVC proposal.[20]

Different types of such noncompetitive behavior has been noted
by the Federal Trade Commission (FTC) in reports[21] that acknowledge
"challenged conduct has included the anticompetitive exclusion of rivals;
the achievement of monopoly power through anticompetitive 'hold
up' tied to standard setting; and the exercise of market power through
reneging on contract terms that reflect standard setting bargains."

In this esoteric space, where the community is extremely small, and
insular, the arguments of exposing such bad behavior and corruption
rest with those that would be most negatively affected by it—in both
reputational arenas as well as competition. And given the very specific
space, it is difficult for other communities to see or understand the level
of misbehavior and its impacts. The issue many times comes down to the
lack of recognition by the participants and the standards organization

---

[19] U.S. Supreme Court. 1988. "Allied Tube v. Indian Head Inc., 486 U.S. 492."
https://supreme.justia.com/cases/federal/us/486/492/ (accessed August 2020).

[20] Organisation for Economic Co-operation and Development, Working Party
#2 on Competition and Regulation. 2010. DAF/COMP/WP2/WD(2010)28.
https://ftc.gov/sites/default/files/attachments/us-submissions-oecd-and-other-
international-competition-fora/usstandardsetting.pdf (accessed August 2020).

[21] Organisation for Economic Co-operation and Development, Working Party
#2 on Competition and Regulation. 2010. DAF/COMP/WP2/WD(2010)28.
https://ftc.gov/sites/default/files/attachments/us-submissions-oecd-and-other-
international-competition-fora/usstandardsetting.pdf (accessed August 2020).

itself of what community is being served, and the resulting battle between which group should have the authority to claim they are promoting the *right way*.

Regarding membership, then:

1. Membership is biased in itself many times; the members themselves typically represent a specific Community of Practice. Where the organization ignores this fact, it results in standards being improperly positioned as *one size fits all*.
2. Membership can be manipulated in where a specific perspective or CoP wields outsized power—typically leveraged to preserve the status quo of existing standards that preserve their own power to the detriment of other communities' needs.
3. It is a challenge for all these organizations to find a perfect structure that would eliminate gamesmanship, or ensure equal representation across multidimensional communities. Alternatively, these organizations should recognize their limitations and biases for specific CoPs, Unfortunately, most are loath to do so, seeing risk in *smaller* membership numbers (and hence, limit their political power).
4. Standards should be specific to Communities of Practice, and focus on how to translate between those Community's standards and languages.

Support Organizations—Industry and Interest-Specific Organizations

Standards Orgs Versus Industry Orgs, and Blurring Lines

Alongside standards organizations, there exist a multitude of *Industry Associations* that tend to be much more community-focused and share common issues. These organizations pursue similar missions in regards to trying to solve for these problems, although they vary in approach and methodology. Some focus on applied solutions—troubleshooting specific issues at the implementation point. Other organizations seek to influence policies, procedures, and at times, regulation and legislation that may impact specific activities. All typically have some aspect of education, as well, looking to share the knowledge, conclusions, and thought leadership from the expertise of its members.

As I discussed in Communities of Practice, and begin to point out the different communities that exist in financial services, it should be no surprise that organizations exist related to those CoPs. From a social and behavioral perspective, it would make sense that members who identify with each other based on roles and purpose would come together for shared goals and experience. Groups like the Bond Dealers Association (BDA), International Swap Dealers Association (ISDA), Association of Global Custodians, the Investment Association, ISITC (formerly the International Securities Association for Institutional Trade Communication), or the National Association of Investment Companies (NAIC), all represent communities that have some shared common identity around the asset class or market role to which they belong.

When these groups are business function-based, they are also many times divided by aspects like jurisdiction. For example, the Investment Association (IA) is UK-based while the NAIC is a U.S.-based organization—both focused on the *buy side* community. Similarly, you have the Loan Market Association (LMA) in the UK, and Loan Syndications and Trading Association (LSTA) in North America. There are broad, jurisdictionally focused organizations, such as Securities Industry and Financial Markets Association (SIFMA), Association for Financial Markets in Europe (AFME) and Brazilian Association of Financial and Capital Market Institutions (ANBIMA), which bring together a super-set of communities for a common goal, mainly in regards to regulation and coordinating interaction with political and regulatory bodies in their jurisdiction. Finally, there are more functional or topic-based organizations like the Enterprise Data Management Council (EDM Council), FinTech Open Source Foundation (FINOS), and Open Data Institute (ODI), that focus on a topic area, such as data, or open source projects. In any case, these all represent communities that exist and have shared needs.

A challenge, however, is when two different organizations need to address the same issue. Outside of the usual politics of organizations believing their organization is always the authoritative voice on any particular subject, there is the factor that in many cases, the organizations involved represent different CoPs. Without much introspection, these organizations, just like standards organizations or any other CoP, can fail to recognize the differences in perspective that may exist between the CoP they represent and those of a different organization that exists on behalf of a different CoP.

Governmental Organizations and Public-Private Partnerships

There are a number of governmental organizations that impact standards, implementation, creation, and usage.

CPMI, IOSCO

The Committee of Payments and Market Infrastructures (CPMI) and the International Organization of Securities Commissions (IOSCO) "work together to enhance coordination of standard and policy development and implementation, regarding clearing, settlement and reporting arrangements including financial market infrastructures (FMIs) worldwide."[22] Consisting of global regulators, central banks, and similar organizations, CPMI-IOSCO has become increasingly active in the standards space, and in recommending various standards to be used or to be created globally across regulatory jurisdictions and regimes. Resolutions are not binding on members, but the organization holds significant authority in directing standards use and market rules. The goals for creating *harmonized* rules and standards is a forward thinking one, and with good intentions. Harmonization, though, is misguided when considering the CoP view. As the basis of this book illustrates, the lack of a CoP nuanced view in such efforts ignores the linguistic variability that is the true barrier to success of this mission.

G30

The Group of 30 (G30) was founded in 1978 and

> is an independent global body comprised of economic and financial leaders from the public and private sectors and academia. It aims to deepen the understanding of global economic and

---

[22] OUCI-IOSCO. 2021. "CPMO IOSCO." *International Organization of Securities Commission.* https://iosco.org/about/?subsection=cpmi_iosco (accessed January 4, 2021).

financial issues, and to explore the international repercussions of decisions taken in the public and private sectors.[23]

It is a very forward looking organization and has published a number of excellent thought leadership papers closely related to the issues explored in this book, although not from a CoP point of view. Indeed, the "Global Clearing and Settlement: A Plan of Action"[24] is an excellent foundation from where I have drawn much.

G20

The Group of 20 (G20), in contrast, brings together governmental and regulatory leaders from 19 countries and the European Union, founded in 1999.[25] Unlike the G30, the G20 is much more policy-focused and more similar to CPMI-IOSCO in membership and purpose. The G20's *Pittsburgh Meeting* in 2008 is often referred to as it occurred on the heels of the market crisis. The Legal Entity Identifier (LEI) standard came out of this group, as did the conceptualization of the Unique Transaction Identifier (UTI) and Unique Product Identifier (UPI) meant to corral and standardize the derivatives industry, seen as the primary cause of the meltdown.

APEC

Organizations like the Asia-Pacific Economic Cooperation (APEC), which focuses on free trade throughout the diverse Asia-Pacific region, are inter-governmental forums focused on trade issues. These groups then cooperate with private industry to host organizations like the APEC Business Advisory Council (ABAC), which

---

[23] Group of 30. 2021. "About the Group of 30." *Group of 30 Consultative Group on International Economics and Monetary Affairs, Inc.* https://group30.org/about (accessed January 4, 2021).

[24] G30Working Group.2003. "Global Clearing and Settlement: A Plan of Action." Report, G30. https://bit.ly/2P5accf. (accessed August 2019).

[25] G20. 2021. "About the G20," https://g20.org/en/about/Pages/default.aspx (accessed January 4, 2021).

provide advice on the implementation of the Osaka Action Agenda and on other specific business sector priorities, and to respond when the various APEC fora request information about business-related issues or to provide the business perspective on specific areas of cooperation.[26]

ABAC then sponsors work under other collectives like the Asia-Pacific Financial Forum (APFF), which focuses on specific initiatives around the region's economy and financial services.

WTO, World Bank, and the like influence, but are typically more involved at the policy level. Like the G20, their policies have profound impact, in some cases, and there is significant disconnect between these organizations and on-the-ground practitioners that need to implement.

Historically Relevant

The Giovaninni Group was a think tank of financial experts in Europe that filed a number of reports with the European Union regarding problems they saw in the industry. Focusing on 15 *barriers*[27] the group was critical of governmental and regulatory policies and legal barriers that impacted efficient markets, in their view. Alberto Giovaninni (1955–2019), the Chair, was a globally recognized economist, and contributed significantly to monetary policy and financial market infrastructure. I make note of this group as their papers, as with the G30, form an excellent foundation to see the issues within financial services. Also, I believe the lack of such a group today, with the authority and experience to both challenge and work alongside global regulators and policymakers, is a detriment to the industry as a whole.

Securities Market Practice Group (SMPG) and the Payments Market Practice Group (PMPG)

---

[26] Asia Pacific Economic Consortium. "Founding and Structure." *APEC Business Advisory Council.* https://www2.abaconline.org//page-content/2521/content (accessed January 4, 2021).

[27] The Giovannini Group. 2002. "Cross-Border Clearing and Settlement Arrangements in the European Union." Economic Papers 163, February, European Commission. URL: https://bit.ly/2J4opk5. (accessed August 2019).

SMPG[28] and the related PMPG[29] are a subset of members from various industry organizations and standards bodies within their individual counties that look to align best practices for the use of various standards, primarily focused on the ISO set of standards. They act as advisory groups for SWIFT in the management of messaging standards over that network.

Conference Organizations

Some groups exist just to put on conferences. While some are merely money-making enterprises, they do provide some function to give platforms for education on various topics. Many, though, are pay-for-play; so many presentations are little more than half hour infomercials for the sponsoring firm or vendor. There are some advantages to these organizations. With their pure focus on organizing events, which funds their staffing, they are able to bring together large populations to attend information sessions regarding industry problems over a number of days. This makes them attractive to senior executives—with events surrounding lavish dinners, daily golf outings, sightseeing trips, open bars, and swanky locations. Networking and entertainment ends up being the priority, as opposed to education. Some are even funded wholly by *sponsors* that want access to make their sales pitch. There have even been programs for three or four day cruises that court executives with the promise of a free vacation, as long as they spend a certain amount of time with a number of the sponsors for their sales presentations each day. The issue here is that these *conferences* get much attention from the press and are held up by those that want to point out the excesses of Wall Street. This takes away attention from the industry organizations, and tends to paint them with the same poor reputation—unfairly in most cases—as well as pulling away money and senior management attention that could fund more applied activities with longer lasting impacts.

---

[28] SMPG. 2021. "About us." *Securities Market Practice Group.* https://smpg.info/index.php?id=3 (accessed January 4, 2021).

[29] SWIFT. 2021. "Payments Market Practice Group." https://swift.com/about-us/community/swift-advisory-groups/payments-market-practice-group (accessed January 4, 2021).

Concerns and Issues With the Standards Process

I began to look into the issues regarding influence and focus regarding membership and constituencies earlier. As noted, regardless of the organization, there is a potential for bad behavior, which can go unchecked. And even when there are efforts to counteract bad behavior, where the bad actor has power—either through money, threat of frivolous lawsuits, reputation, or political capital—it is rarely addressed or resolved.

The participating constituency is critical to consider. With over 100 countries potentially in a committee, with multiple representatives for each country, an ISO standards development process can easily become unwieldy. There may be over weighted participation from one member country, or a group of member countries. Or there may be very limited participation in small niche community. Given the expansiveness of the financial services world, if there is an imbalance in subject matter focus at the national level, this will be further highlighted in any ISO work. Some of this lack of expertise is expected to be countered by liaison participation, but this is not always the case.

When the standard being worked on is a focused, specific standard, this isn't necessarily an issue. However, if the standard is meant to be more general, this can become problematic. If it is positioned as being for a general purpose or community larger than that creating it, the lack of expertise likely will not be noticed until too late. Unintended bias is an ignored issue as a standard passes through a process. Further, once a standard is *in the wild*, there is little critical examination of it by those recommending the implementation and use of the standard. Moreover there can be a natural (and incorrect) assumption that there was a rigorous and expansive evaluation during the development process.

This is not to say that all standards suffer from this. And even in these cases, the participants are usually contributing the expertise they do have in an open and honest manner. While there may be ways to counter these issues, some are harder to address than others. Meanwhile, admitting or acknowledging that these problems exist, even if they are a minority of cases, can undermine existing standards and the ongoing good work. Counter to this, however, is that a mis-applied standard can introduce systemic risk into the financial system. We can relate this to our hypothetical case of the silver bullet. A community that has battled werewolves in the past, that tries to push its silver bullet solution on a community dealing with vampires misses out on the nuance that this new problem presents. This can cause much harm during a campaign to elevate their standard as the *more right* solution, out of ignorance and lack of expertise.

Some of the difficulty is driven by the fact that most of this work is volunteer-driven. Tied to the funding issue—companies need to weigh the benefits of having some of their top talent/minds, spending time—some significantly—on standards work not directly tied to the company's bottom line, and with an opaque or indirect ROI. And those volunteers must navigate the politics of having a *day job* versus doing *pro bono* work for the different industry standards groups to which they may belong.

Bias also is introduced due to different funding models. There is an argument that firms with more financial interest can, and will, *pay up* for the more influential memberships, in order to be eligible for broad participation, as opposed to actual subject matter experts better suited to the work. By influencing the process with their own particular viewpoint, any standards created will unnaturally favor that company's viewpoints, methodologies, and potentially technologies. And as noted previously, there is the reality that organizations with a monetary vested interest, the desire to protect a monopoly, or otherwise restrict competition can and will corrupt or otherwise hijack the standards process to their benefit, There is little recourse, and no public knowledge, even by those implementing policies that adopt or incorporate those standards, of the potential corruption.

In the end, standards are needed. Their benefits outweigh much of the negative. But that doesn't mean downsides should be ignored or brushed to the side. Where the negative effects are felt, there needs to be more action to address those problems. No system is infallible, and the approach of just making it work and fixing things later can lead to more harm than good. Once something is in process, it is rarely changed or adjusted. Community is given a passing mention (i.e., a common complaint being that an organization needs more participation from the *buy side* or from the *sell side*), but driving interest for participation from diverse communities many times leads to a dilution of the value proposition and relevance for one or more of the communities who participates.

Standards in Financial Services

Some Relevant Standards in ISO

ISO 7775/ISO 15022/ISO 20022 are standards that influence the discussion about communication, data, definitions, and ultimately our concerns about approaches in standards ignoring Communities of Practice. Given the intertwined nature of these three ISO standards, it makes sense to cover them together, following their evolution from a historical perspective. A good companion book would be "SWIFT: Cooperative Governance for Network Innovation, standards and community" by Susan V. Scott and Marcos Zachariadis. Some of the following history behind ISO 7775 references this excellent book.

ISO 7775—"Triple Seven Five" was the original messaging protocol created by SWIFT, and then translated into an ISO standard.[30] The transition to ISO occurred over time, as influence from Swiss Banks already invested in SWIFT looked to prevent duplication and redundancy being pursued within ISO TC68. Interestingly enough, the decision to move toward ISO was to include a larger community than incorporated SWIFT members. (Fast forward to 2020 and there is an effort to create a group outside of ISO because participation is too restricted, and SWIFT is limited in its ability to intervene).

By the mid 1990s, ISO 7775 was effectively 25 years old as a messaging format, and had evolved little. This lack of evolution is typically attributed to the standards' inflexible nature and the biased focus on the processing of custodian banks that originally led the message creation efforts, as noted by Jamie Shay, of SWIFT, during that time.

> ... [W]e were sometimes accused in standards of developing messages that people couldn't use ... and this is what happened in securities ... there was a difference in opinion as to what needed to be in the messages and there was a feeling that we [SWIFT]

---

[30] Scott, S.V., and M. Zachariadis. 2013. *SWIFT: Cooperative Governance for Network Innovation, Standards and Community*, 66. New York, NY: Routledge.

were developing messages without really consulting that side of the business, because we created these messages by talking to banks, when in fact 'buys' and 'sell', etc. are done by brokers and asset managers.[31]

ISO 15022 promised to separate the message structure and format from the business meaning. Issued in March 1999, the work had begun years prior, and focused on creating independent business objects not specifically linked to a particular message and therefore could easily be reused. It leveraged the existing SWIFT syntax of field tags with specific definitions but with flexible presentation options. In addition, an inventory of *ISO 7775 replacement* messages were included. Whereas ISO 7775 was a standard that described specific messages and their formal structure, ISO 15022 defined the business objects and suggested messages. The difference being—if a new message was needed in ISO 7775 (or even an existing message needed changes), the entire standard required revision—a long and drawn out process. In contrast, the message structure in ISO 15022 was outside of the standard itself, allowing SWIFT to introduce new messages and make changes to message structure without needing to reopen the actual standard, except for items that did not explicitly exist or objects that required revision.

During that time, W3C had been developing XML, which was issued in 1998. Due to this overlapping, and the rapid shift in technology focus to TCP/IP, network technologies, and the resulting adoption of XML as an open standard, effort began almost immediately to focus on translating ISO 15022 into a version that utilized XML syntax and presentation. As that work progressed, Jamie Shay of SWIFT noted the call for creating a single common standard that would cover all of the financial industry was raised.

WG10's commitment to building a durable unified standard scheme to service the entire supply chain and provide

---

[31] Scott, S.V., and M. Zachariadis. 2013. *SWIFT: Cooperative Governance for Network Innovation, Standards and Community*, 66. New York, NY: Routledge.

interoperability across wholesale financial markets and other industry sectors led committee members to rethink the 15022 XML initiative. The call to ensure that "this time, these standards should be for all types of messages, not only securities" prevailed "and the standard was moved up to TC68 level" to include all banking, securities and related financial services operations.[32]

This was, arguably, a very bold statement. At the time, the industry was in a global experiment to create a 'Global Straight Through Processing' system (GSTPA), that would centralize all trading and settlement activity (i.e., centralize the supply chain). In addition, data centralization and creation of *golden source* databases were the trending solution for data issues across enterprises.

From an applied linguistics perspective, however, the statement and goal—especially in hindsight—raises many questions. Goals conflict with perspective, such as wishing to service the entire supply chain—yet clearly working from an *operations* perspective. The desire to apply to *other industry sectors* is both murky and aspirational. It would be fair to question if there was sufficiently diverse and deep enough expertise within the working group to accomplish such a task.

ISO 20022 was developed and published in 2004. Adoption remained difficult, given that most firms had just expended significant money on converting from ISO 7775 to ISO 15022, and were yet to experience any ROI. Through the 2008 financial crisis, ISO 20022 remained on the fringes until the G20 report, and a concerted lobbying campaign by ISO 20022 experts and supporters with regulators, mostly European, to adopt *standards* and specifically 20022, as a way to solve the problems underlying the 2008 market issues. This campaign leveraged the name of ISO to foster more legitimacy, and by association conferred even more *prestige status* to the ISO brand.

ISO20022 as it currently stands is more akin to a large data dictionary than a business model, although from an applied linguistics point of view, this is not a bad thing. Certainly, having a dictionary is a primary

---

[32] Scott, S.V., and M. Zachariadis. 2013. *SWIFT: Cooperative Governance for Network Innovation, Standards and Community*, 70. New York, NY: Routledge.

need to begin the exploration on differences in meaning (or alignment in meaning) across different CoPs. However, a dictionary is not authoritative nor does it encompass the whole of all language across communities—only whatever portions of language contributing communities have registered. That is to say, if a community has not contributed, then its language and definitions have not been included. Further, a dictionary does not indicate how to use language, or what definition for a term is the right definition given any particular circumstance—even if there is an associated business model.

As an example, we can look at the word *lead*. If just given the word, and asked for the right usage—without any other guiding context, it would be impossible to understand what the word intended. And without hearing how it was pronounced (long or short 'e'), the divergence between being a soft metal or some type of concept grows even more stark. The word can be used as a verb, noun, or adjective. Even if used in a sentence, there could be room from ambiguity. This stems from the fact that the linguistic sign is arbitrary.

If we limit the usage to within a specific CoP, however, it is likely that the meaning will be readily determined, without any accompanying guidance or context. The likelihood that the use of *lead* in a community of metallurgists or in a water purification system refers to the metal becomes much more certain.

The word L-E-A-D

Lead verb (1) \ ˈlēd \ **led**\ ˈled \; **leading**
Definition of *lead* (Entry 1 of 5)
transitive verb
1a: to guide on a way especially by going in advance *led* the officers to his hiding place
  b: to direct on a course or in a direction a road *leading* the traveler to the heart of the city
  c: to serve as a channel for a pipe *leads* water to the house
2: to go through : *lead* a quiet life
3a(1): to direct the operations, activity, or performance of *lead* an orchestra

(2): to have charge of *lead* a campaign

(3): to suggest to (a witness) the answer desired by asking leading questions counsel is *leading* this witness, putting words in her mouth— Erle Stanley Gardner

b(1): to go at the head of *lead* a parade

(2): to be first in or among *lead* the league

(3): to have a margin over *led* his opponent

4: to bring to some conclusion or condition *led* to believe otherwise

5: to begin play with *lead* trumps

6a: to aim in front of (a moving object)*lead* a duck

b: to pass a ball or puck just in front of (a moving teammate)

intransitive verb

1a: to guide someone or something along a way You *lead* and we'll follow.

b: to lie, run, or open in a specified place or direction path *leads* uphill

c: to guide a dance partner through the steps of a dance

2a: to be first This state *leads* in population.

b(1): BEGIN, OPEN will *lead* off with a Christmas story— Richard Bissell

(2): to play the first card of a trick, round, or game

3: to tend toward or have a result study *leading* to a degree

4: to direct the first of a series of blows at an opponent in boxing

lead one down the garden path *or less commonly* **lead one up the garden path**

: HOODWINK, DECEIVE I'd rather he be disappointed with the truth rather than *lead him down the garden path*— Harold Robbins

Lead noun (1) \ ˈlēd \

Definition of *lead* (Entry 2 of 5)

1a(1): LEADERSHIP look to the president for a unifying *lead*— D. W. Brogan

(2): EXAMPLE, PRECEDENT followed the *lead* of the majority leader in voting

b(1): position at the front **:** VANGUARD The runner from Kenya was in the *lead* for most of the race.

(2): INITIATIVE took the *lead* in fighting the measure

(3): the act or privilege of playing first in a card game. Your partner has the *lead*. *Also* **:** the card or suit played first. His *lead* was the ace.

c: a margin or measure of advantage or superiority or position in advance enjoys a good *lead* over all competitors

2: one that leads: such as

a: LODE sense 2

b: a channel of water especially through a field of ice

c: INDICATION, CLUE The detectives had a few *leads* to follow.

d: a principal role in a dramatic production. She was the romantic *lead* in the movie. *also* **:** one who plays such a role

e: LEASH sense 1 train a dog to walk on a *lead*

f(1): an introductory section of a news story **:** LEDE edit the *lead* to grab the reader's attention

  (2): a news story of chief importance. The story of his arrest was the *lead* in newspapers across the country.

3: an insulated electrical conductor connected to an electrical device

4: the course of a rope from end to end

5: the amount of axial (see AXIAL sense 2a) advance of a point accompanying a complete turn of a thread (as of a screw or worm)

6: a position taken by a base runner off a base toward the next. The runner on first took a big *lead*.

7: the first punch of a series or an exchange of punches in boxing

Lead adjective \ 'led \

Definition of *lead* (Entry 3 of 5)

: acting or serving as a lead (see LEAD entry 2) or leader a *lead* article

Lead noun (2), often attributive \ 'led \

Definition of *lead* (Entry 4 of 5)

1: a soft, heavy, metallic element with atomic number 82 found mostly in combination and used especially in alloys, batteries, and shields against sound, vibration, or radiation— see CHEMICAL ELEMENTS TABLE

2a: a plummet for sounding at sea

 b: leads *plural, British* **:** a usually flat lead roof

 c: leads *plural* **:** lead framing for panes in windows

d: a thin strip of metal used to separate lines of type in printing

3a: a thin stick of marking substance (such as graphite) in or for a pencil

 b: WHITE LEAD

4: BULLETS, PROJECTILES

5: TETRAETHYL LEAD

Lead verb (2) \ 'led \ **leaded; leading; leads**

Definition of *lead* (Entry 5 of 5)

transitive verb

1: to cover, line, or weight with lead (see LEAD entry 4)

2: to fix (window glass) in position with leads

3: to put space between the lines of (typeset matter)

4: to treat or mix with lead or a lead compound *leaded* gasoline[33]

With ISO 20022, this certainty is suspect at best. Given the variability of communities within financial services, there is less certainty that any given term will have a consistent meaning across those communities. Further, any group can come in with a new business justification and add a new, slightly different, definition to the list. Nor would it be right to insist that all communities accept any single definition that another group had placed in the dictionary. Viewing the standard from a community of practice viewpoint; then what should be the community bounds for ISO 20022? More so, what is the community, or communities, that created and contributed to it, and how do they relate, interact (or not) with other communities that are expected to adopt and use it? In the end, we have an arbitrary dictionary, written by a specific CoP, yet is assumed, incorrectly, to be the authoritative language of the financial services community.

FIX Protocol and FpML—A Different Approach Than ISO?

Some standards start as a common need identified in a particular group or community, which then becomes a life of its own. They become de facto

[33] Merriam-Webster Online, *lead* https://merriam-webster.com/dictionary/lead (accessed August 2019).

standards, first by agreement of a group of players in the industry with enough gravitas to encourage adoption

FIX, in contrast to ISO, is a community-led organization, funded by its members, as opposed to ISO that is focused on selling standards within its library, and only working with designated National Standards Bodies. FIX focuses on the messaging protocol for efficient communication between its community members. The FIX Protocol and FIXML are the actual standards that enable both the creation of FIX standard messages, and a transmission protocol for sending those messages over various technologies.

FpML, on the other hand, is managed by ISDA. ISDA's community is even more specific than the FIX community, given the pure focus on derivative products. ISDA operates a number of working groups that look to update and maintain FpML for the electronic communication of derivatives-related trading and process needs.

Identification Standards

FIX, ISO 15022 and FpML are all what would be considered *messaging* standards. They incorporate the language of their communities, and structure the messages in a way that makes it consistent within one CoP or another. However, the underlying function of financial markets is to transact something with some entity. So, it would make sense that there is a way to identify those things and those entities.

What the reader should expect by now is that there are many different ways that instruments and entities are identified—indeed how they are defined.

From an instrument perspective, CoP drives much of the identifier of choice. Traders require the ability to see a short bit of data that they can quickly mentally process and remember, as well as codes that are short so they can type them into screens and systems quickly. Tickers tend to be the dominant type of identifier, although they are not standardized across the industry. Ticker schemes are typically standardized by specific exchange, or data vendor, though in some cases financial jurisdictions like Singapore have created a national standard representation.

Tickers are then usually specific to a certain exchange or data vendor. So many tickers may exist in a single country that has only one CSD (remember from Chapter 2). It would not be efficient to have the middle office, or back office community using tickers to match across counterparties or effect settlement. Different firms may have different data vendors, or executions for the same instrument may have been done across different exchanges and bulked into a single average price trade. So, national standards like CUSIP, or other national ID's like Singapore's national ID are used, or the ISIN (a global ISO standard) when dealing with a single local market.

In a cross-border transaction, however, both sides need to know what country the instrument is due to settle in. So using a code like the SEDOL or FIGI provides the context needed that includes the country where an instrument is officially listed (OPOL), settles, and the currency it prices in, and ignores the place of trade that only the trader front office community is concerned about. FIGI, unlike other older identifier standards, actually also provides a referential data model to link other standards together across contexts and communities. In the end, there are hundreds, if not thousands of different identifier types for just financial instruments. Some believe that this should not be, and there should only be one. However, linguistically, I would instead invoke that there is no right or wrong, and that CoP need drives this diversity.

This illustrates the different language different CoPs use, and how it impacts communication across the industry. While all these identifiers identify an *instrument*, the data that is associated with that *object* differs depending on the different functional CoPs involved, even though it is the same *thing*.

Other De Facto Standards

Some standards become standards due to being first movers or innovators that become embedded into the everyday processes of the industry, as we saw with FpML. Across and within CoPs, the standards are too numerous to go into detail here. The existence of multiple accounting standards, alone, would likely take a complete volume. There are standards specific to asset class, to functions, and firm types. But there is little attention paid to formally defining these communities, recognizing their unique-ness, how they interact, intersect, and overlay each other.

Standards Overlay With Community

In financial services, the needs for standards can be broken down into four somewhat arbitrary groupings; representation, transport, definition, and consumption. With these groupings, we can look at how CoPs differ and interact across that *type* of standard, express why there are more than one standard, and how that impacts the industry.

By representation, I mean the protocol or basic form, technically that is used. This is less strictly financial services, and likely falls more on the technical end of the scale. But I refer to XML, tag-based, Excel or .csv, and UML. There are plenty of others. But these tend to be some of the basic representation tools used in the later transport, definition, and consumption of data. What differentiates use is usually the technological sophistication of the firm or user, the age of the technology or system, or even the standard and how it was built.

Transport sits squarely on top of representation, and revolves around messaging. The type of information being interchanged—if it is transactional, or informational—affects the transport needs. Some information requires low latency—speed of information being critical, while other information may be less dependent temporally. Many times the standards for transport (FIX, ISO 15022/20022, FpML) do not actually define how to use them properly in a *standard* way, such that the same information can end up looking like two completely different messages, even when using the same standard.

Definition refers to classification, identification, relationships, and dictionary concepts. What is the type of thing that needs defining? How do you then identify it, within the right context, for the right CoP? What is its relationship to other things? Are the relationships hierarchical or more complex, and can a taxonomy or ontology help? Dictionary concepts become important, as we discussed earlier with the l-e-a-d example. What does it mean when we say something like *End of Day Price*?

Finally, consumption refers to both taking and displaying data and information. Again, back to a systems view in some regards, there is the need to understand if consumption is happening on a mainframe versus a web platform—or across both. What are the impacts of transport and definition on the needs in consumption? Is there a recursive issue—for example, mainframes are notoriously difficult to change, so if a new *thing* requires a field to be expanded to enable its definition, that could have significant impacts. Choice of vendors can be a tradeoff between functionality and depth of information or flexibility.

For our purposes, we are most concerned with Definition and Consumption. These are the two major items where a focus on CoPs can provide the most utility, and help reshape how we approach creating solutions and standards.

Just the concept of an individual, as we see in Figure 11.2, is dependent upon the purpose, why they are being described or referenced. One aspect from applied linguistics that comes up here is arbitrariness.

A key concept in linguistics was advocated by Saussure, following Whitney, that the linguistic sign is arbitrary. This is the arbitrariness property, and it is one of the nine design features of natural language listed by Charles Hockett. Arbitrariness in this case means that the form of a linguistic expression is in general unconnected to its meaning. In other words, one cannot predict the meaning of an expression from its form. This is relevant to language change, because since form and meaning are not intrinsically bound, one can change without the other. This allows languages to change. When members of a linguistic sub-community talk to each other, they tend to fashion a sub-dialect to make their communication more efficient. But in the process, this leaves non-members out, who are unable to participate fully in the sub-dialect. For examples, doctors talking to other doctors, or ear-nose-and-throat specialists talking to other ear-nose-and-throat specialists.[34]

What we find in Figure 11.2 is that the very basic concept of a *person* is itself arbitrary. The CoP concerned with pets, may take the expression of a person to mean a relationship to the type of pet they own. Meanwhile, a community interested in family history will express in regards to where someone sits in the family tree, and a business looks to those expressions of an individual as it relates to their status as an employee.

Why are standards so complex in financial servicex?
Try to describe a single person, different perspectives;

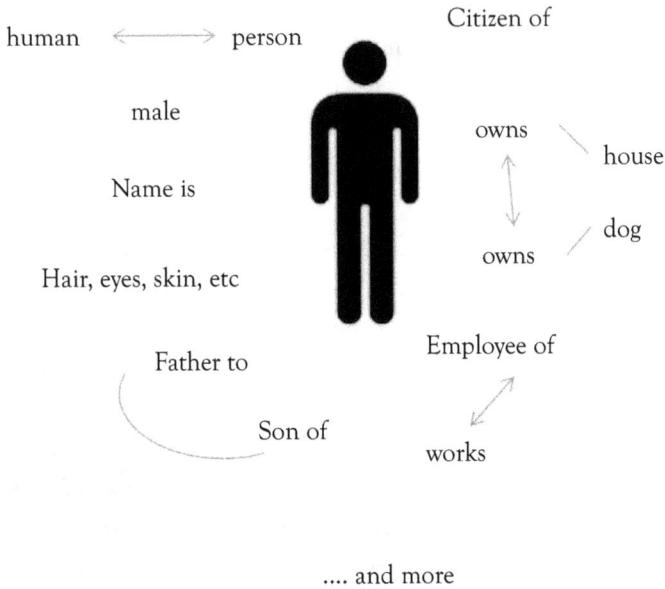

Figure 11.2 *Person and standards*

Dean Werner's example of different doctors gives another view into this. One would not expect a pediatrician to hold a detailed discussion on oncology simply because all involved are doctors. In the same way, in financial services, brokers discussing a trade are likely not discussing the same expression of a trade that a custodian settling a trade at a depository would be expressing. The concept of the expression is embedded within the context—the community—in which it is being expressed.

---

[34] Werner, Thomas, Dean, Linguistics, Carnegie Mellon University (2019). E-mail message to author.

Standards Fighting With Themselves

How standards align with certain communities... and that's not a bad thing...

A good case study to look at that highlights the lack of awareness of CoPs is the contrast between FIX and ISO standards. This is only one of the easier examples, but it is not the only instance of where standards organizations, and different CoPs end up fighting each other. The most visible confusion between standards in financial services may be between FIX and ISO formats. This conflict ties back into the lack of recognition of CoPs between front and back offices, and in some cases Fixed Income versus Equity. FIX was borne out of the need for front offices to communicate with each other for the trading of assets, between sell-side firms.

ISO formats, as discussed, addressed the needs of buy-side firms to communicate with their custodians, as well as with their dealers—traditionally mid and back office. Even membership in the various standards groups clearly illustrates this dichotomy, with different individuals from the same institutions attending the various groups based on function they perform—the community they identify with most within their firm. You would be hard pressed to find a trader or other front office professional at an ISITC conference, for example.

The lack of clearly understanding Communities of Practice, by both the individuals supporting particular solutions, as well as the organization they use to advance those agendas perpetuates the perceived *conflict*, *competition* and *overlap* among these standards. This is fed, in part, by the aforementioned vilifying of *silos* within firms instead of creating acceptance that each different community is valid and focus should instead be on interoperability and translation.

Both ISO and FIX muddy the waters through offering *competing* messaging in the pretrade, allocation, and post-trade spaces, mostly in response to the demands of their membership. Also, they fall into the trap of assuming their communities are the same—from settlement instructions and confirmation processes to market data and asset class coverage. While there is overlap, there is less focus on highlighting where the communities differ as opposed to what amounts to land-grabbing. Some of this ties to the not-for-profit organizations connected to these standards,

SWIFT and FPL, among other organizations that have a financial vested interest in expanding the status quo. However, as industry-funded not-for-profits, more effort needs to be made by their disparate memberships to coordinate rather than compete.

To be fair, these organizations and others have stood up and agreed in principle to work together over the years, as illustrated by the Investment Roadmap. But they are also driven by their constituencies, which span multiple CoPs, which are driven by real business needs that require solutions sooner rather than later, leveraging existing investments. However, it is notable that their constituencies, as previously stated, come from the same organizations. The same firm has multiple individuals, that belong to different standards organizations that are in turn advocating and championing different solutions as the one *true* solution above the others. This is blamed on silos and politics, but with a CoP view, we can better provide a path for understanding and cooperation.

To date, both FIX and ISO seem to make stuttered progress in working together. This is also true in regards to other standards organizations, depending on the interaction point. OMG, for example, has fairly good relationship with ISO's JTC1 committee, but that does not extend across all of ISO TC's. And interactions between CoPs typically comes with some level of mistrust and bias. The industry view that these, and other, organizations try to take is often hampered by vocal members who are passionate, yet partisan. These partisan members continue to push a message of competition among standards, and that there are *overlapping* spaces of pre trade, trade, and post trade, and only *their* standard deserves the continued expansion and competition in these spaces. This is not unique to these organizations, but is representative of a recurring issue amongst most industry organizations. The primary focus for each organization are for different CoPs, but the conflict comes in where these CoPs naturally meet and need to interact—yet do not recognize their differences. At these points, translation and interoperability should be the focus, whereas instead, each individual CoP claims sole domain, or insists on a lowest common denominator *consensus* approach that everyone— even those not relevant—weigh in.

Standards organizations need to meet together and to specifically and clearly define where each group operates as CoPs. While there may be agreement with some fundamentals among standards leadership, there remains extensive confusion in the industry. The industry needs clear decisions that do not preserve the status quo, but provide crisp delineation between the various standards scope and remit; for example, the specific Community of Practice the standard applies to. More attention needs to be paid to mapping out the various spaces where, as an industry, we can agree that a particular standard should be used—by asset type and process (trade, post-trade, etc.).

The truth is that there are significant firms that have a vested interest in particular standards. People have volunteered years of their lives to standards, not to mention companies' investment in infrastructure to support one standard or another. Often times, individuals from the same company sit on opposite sides of the fence in promoting competing standards, even with completely separate infrastructures within an organization.

Harmonization and interoperability does not mean that multiple standards exist side-by-side, performing the same exact function for the same CoP. Nor does it mean that one standard should be adopted above all others across all existing CoPs. It should mean to us that standards exist for specific purposes, within a specific CoP. And when moving from one purpose to the next, handing off from one process to the next, from one Community of Practice to the next, those standards should be able to interoperate. Expediency should not lead to shoe-horning improper standards into place.

Vendors and industry utilities need to recognize this, as well. Increasingly, vendors and utilities have begun to add support for use of different standards—from FIX to FpML as primary formats into their products over the use of proprietary means. This is a good thing. FIX, ISO, XBRL, FpML and other standards are all very important to the continued operation and growth of the industry. But if standards organizations continue to support creation of mandates, regulation and legislation to benefit their standard over others, regardless of CoP, they act in a way that is counterproductive to their primary mission.

To be fair, FIX has some self-awareness around its mission, openness, and defining its scope. This would be boosted by viewing their mission through the lens of Communities of Practice to better define their messaging. The implications currently are that those FIX and other organizations speak to do not listen through that context. Messaging outward does not first create that bounding box, clearly articulating what is in and out of the community. This is because the tools to help create these CoP definitions are not used in financial services—applied linguistics is not a discipline used in the industry. The expertise to first speak about Communities of Practice and applied linguistics does not exist in this space, especially within standards organizations. As we will explore, regulators and legislators, journalists, and other industry players therefore *hear* that standards exist as an overarching one-size-fits-all, silver bullet solution.

Without using the tools within applied linguistics to better nuance this, it is doubtful that this misreading and misapplication of standards will cease being a problem. Standards are held up as an example of how to reduce operational risk. How they can be leveraged to bring disparate data sources together for better information analysis. How they help eliminate manual processing and errors ranging from the many semantic definitions of *End of Day Price* to the complex modeling of an OTC derivatives product. Unless standards and their supporters truly begin to play nice in the sandbox with each other and industry utilities, they are instead going to be a constant source of risk, confusion, and unnecessary cost.

Standards Wrap-Up

I have spent considerable time on standards because standards work is a critical intersection point where recognizing Communities of Practice would have the most impact. Standards organizations do tend to naturally gravitate to certain CoPs, which makes sense. However, even in those cases, standards participants have also created new CoPs, specific to those that work in standards. Where these standards CoPs cross broad areas such as ISO's TC68, they consistently ignore the diversity of financial CoP's they impact, the bias of standards overruling. Where a standards CoP is a sub community of another CoP, such as FIX is with the front office, there can be a struggle to see the boundaries with other CoPs.

Technology confuses this interaction even more, promising that using technology to utilize a standard will enable its broad application, use and consumption by all (ignoring our Infology principles that not all data is for everyone). The pure focus on data forgets the fact that all data is not equal—that trade is not necessarily a trade. The constant search for a silver bullet—boosted by lowest common denominator consensus agreement—only drives toward acceptance by a majority where the least feathers will be ruffled, not necessarily solving the actual problem for the specific CoP that may exist. Further, in solving for one CoP, the silver bullet method seeks to solve for all the CoPs in one fell swoop, and focuses more on convincing those communities that silver bullets will kill vampires.

This has been boosted in recent years, especially since the G20's stumbling into the standards wars in 2008. Regulators have become much more active in standards, and while that is a good thing, it belies their outsized voice and influence as a CoP, which we will explore in the following chapter. This presence also has not been coupled with a strong enough counterweight that works in concert with the regulatory CoP—mainly because a lack of trust, bias, and power conflicts regulators have with the different CoP's explored in Chapters 5 through 7.

Standards organizations, and the industry organizations that support them, then, need to help in stepping back, and clearly identifying the existence of different CoPs. Some of this work is happening in the OMG, as well as the semantic working group at ISO/TC68, but not on a formal basis, and a sustainable methodology has not been found or applied. This is most because of the lack of expertise among standards participants in applied linguistics and the concepts around CoPs, and the inherent biases that exist among the participants. This is in most cases not intentional, rather it is expected given the behavior of CoPs and the impact on language and understanding cross-CoP.

In closing, on standards:

- Standards are critical to efficient, safe, transparent functioning financial markets
- The approach to standards, to date, is problematic because it has assumed and promoted singular standards as universally applicable, as opposed to specific to certain communities
- Standard setters also have a blind spot toward different CoP's, due to, in many cases, expert bias.

- Without proper recognition of the various CoP's in the industry, application of standards (forced or otherwise) can lead to just as much harm as the lack of any standard.
- Standards should be create by, and applied within, specific CoPs.
- A new set of sponsored activity should focus on the interoperability between CoP focused standards, through the applied linguistics lens, involving the target CoP as well as regulatory or policy making participation.

CHAPTER 12

The Regulatory Community

Global regulators and governments have increasingly referred to creation or standardization of a common financial language as the best solution to the woes facing the financial industry. In December 2017, the European Commission launched a public consultation that refers to the development of a common financial language.[1] Previous to that, the Commission's FDS Project refers to the lack of a common financial language.[2] This topic was raised again at the "Preparing Supervisory Reporting for the Digital Age" EU Commission Conference in Brussels on June 4, 2018.[3] It is also represented in the expansive work done on the Global Legal Entity Identifier since 2008, as well as in the United States within the Office of Financial Research (OFR) that was formed as a result of the Dodd-Frank Act. Backed by the nirvana promised by *standardization*, this common-sense approach appears very logical on its face, without the consideration of CoPs. In 2012, Andrew Haldane presented the paper "Towards a common financial language" specifically on this concept of a universal financial language (Haldane 2012). Since then, it has become a regular talking point for regulators, standards organizations, and others trying to rationalize the financial industry.

---

[1] European Commission. 2018. "Summary Report of the Public Consultation on the Fitness Check on Supervisory Reporting having taken place from December 1, 2017 to March 14, 2018." https://ec.europa.eu/info/sites/info/files/2017-supervisory-reporting-requirements-summary-report_en.pdf (accessed January 2021).

[2] European Commission. 2016. "Towards Better Financial Data Reporting." https://ec.europa.eu/isa2/actions/towards-better-financial-data-reporting_en (accessed August 2020).

[3] European Commission. 2018. "Conference: Preparing Supervisory Reporting for the Digital Age." https://ec.europa.eu/info/events/finance-180604-supervisory-reporting_en (accessed January 4, 2021).

What should be clear to the reader at this point, however, is that the adoption of a single European or global financial language—while frequently raised by policy makers as a means for promoting operational efficiency and reducing the burden of regulatory compliance in financial services—is not practically achievable. It is simply far too large, complex, and costly a task. More so, it ignores the basic reality of the CoP presence and the associate linguistic implications presented previously.

While the FDS project later clarifies an approach based on frameworks and interoperability, most discussions and approaches remain more simplistic. There lacks inclusion of a formal linguistic methodology and understanding within regulators' projects and plans. As we have explored in this book, a "Common Financial Language" where a single standard language is adopted across all facets of the industry, is not really feasible. The reality of multiple, overlapping, and complex Communities of Practice belies the simplicity that the regulatory community wishes to impose. I do not lay complete blame at their feet, however. Regulators can only be as informed as those advising them. In some regulatory communities, there is a distinct bias toward those in the standards community as opposed to a level of mistrust of voices coming from the various industry-based organizations and individuals. And there does not seem to be any knowledge or inclusion of linguistics. However, Regulators and policy/law makers hold an outsized influence on use (and misuse), application of, and success (or not) of standards. At the same time, regulators, policy and law makers are typically not experts (nor can they be) across the industry landscape and have less awareness of the different CoPs.

The G30 (A Plan of Action 2003),[4] and Giovannini (2001)[5] before them, advocated that "This would provide for inter-operability between national systems and could allow for a choice of systems to be used at each stage of a securities transaction" (Giovannini) and "the overall benefits of

[4] G30 Working Group. 2003. "Global Clearing and Settlement: A Plan of Action." https://group30.org/publications/detail/123 (accessed January 4, 2021).
[5] Giovannini Group. 2001. "Cross-Border Clearing and Settlement Arrangements in the European Union." https://ec.europa.eu/info/publications/giovannini-reports_en (accessed August 2020).

full interoperability will eventually be greater than the sum of these parts." (G30), that is, *parts* being individual standards efforts. The G30 Report took a much broader, global, viewpoint than that of Giovannini, but both reports clearly reflect the understanding that there could not be a single solution to the problems of language and interpretation, and that regulators alone could not address many of these issues—important points that seem to have been overlooked in recent years. In fact, Giovannini was clear that regulators should focus on resolving the legal definitions that cause conflict across jurisdictions, as opposed to business processes and identification standards.[6] Even more important, is the point to allow choice. While Gionannini likely did not have CoPs in mind, it is intuitively clear that those involved in the report recognized that there were distinct communities with different needs that should be allowed to choose their own solutions, as long as interoperability was pursued. The G30 Plan of Action remains a viable blueprint, though in need of some updating integrating concepts from this book, and papers from other academics regarding applied linguistics, language, and standards that are referenced herein. Contextual standards and interoperability would seem to be where more energy should be spent, rather than the efforts to standardize language on the whole.

This is not to ignore efforts going on in the industry around context and community that are focused toward governments and regulators. OMG is sponsoring a number of working groups around Standardized Business Reporting Models[7] aimed toward machine-readable business reporting, Federated Enterprise Risk Management,[8] around U.S. Government data initiatives, and the Vocabularies for Community of Interest,[9] specifically

[6] Giovannini Group. 2001. "Cross-Border Clearing and Settlement Arrangements in the European Union." https://ec.europa.eu/info/publications/giovannini-reports_en, pg. 60 (accessed August 2020).

[7] Object Management Group. 2020. "Standard Business Report Model." *OMG Wiki.* https://omgwiki.org/SBRM/doku.php (accessed January).

[8] Object Management Group. 2020. "FIRM: Federated Enterprise Risk Management WG." *OMG Wiki.* https://omgwiki.org/FERM/doku.php (accessed January 4, 2021).

[9] Object Management Group. 2020. "Vocabularies for communities of interest," *OMG Wiki.* https://omgwiki.org/vcoi/doku.php (January 4, 2021).

discussing topics relevant to context and communities. Similarly, ISO TC68's Subcommittee 9 has an ongoing Working Group regarding technology and semantics that has a collection of experts, with some cross-pollination represented on both groups. There is, however, still a lack of wider representation, especially from the regulatory community. The impact of this is that the complexities and issues of data are discussed and more understood within these small groups, but those making policy are not aware. Policies and regulatory expectations, then, reflect a very simplistic view that does not incorporate the complexities and learnings on context and communities in regards to applying standards in data. As vast and complex standard organizations and other similar groups are in financial services, the regulatory community can be vastly more harrowing. As mentioned before, just within the United States, former Commissioner Gallagher showcased his a *crazy quilt* of regulation in financial services. Regulators serve a key role in financial services—ensuring transparency, access to markets, fairness, preventing abuse, looking to foster efficiency and competition, as well as serving the goals of their specific jurisdictions—whether those as a local municipality, a state or province, a country, or an economic collective like the European Union.

And many regulators understand the complexities and the resulting challenges that exist in financial services. The Bank of England's "Future of Post Trade" white paper states:

> Post-trade processes, both within and across firms, have evolved organically over time, with layers of legacy technology systems, infrastructures, and workflows. The resulting patchwork, while functional, is complex, costly and inefficient—which impacts operational resilience. As just one example, data are not always standardized and are held in multiple systems that may require constant reconciliation, raising costs and the chance of errors. Taken together across the trade life cycle, across all asset classes, and across all firms, the inefficiencies in post-trade processes present both a significant opportunity for change, and a source of systemic risk.[10]

---

[10] "Future of Post Trade" https://bankofengland.co.uk/-/media/boe/files/report/2020/the-future-of-post-trade-report.pdf?la=en&hash=825A6A6DCF9810BA7258FCB3B2FABEAD081DD42B (accessed July 2020).

Yet, still in many ways, regulators, regulation, and legislators are stuck in the past, forever looking at *what should be* versus the reality of the overall system, and that most parts of that system speak a different language than they do. H.L. Mencken begins with a discussion on how professors of English language ignored American dialect, having "worked steadily toward a highly artificial formalism, and as steadily against the investigation of the actual national speech." In many ways, the insistence on standards across financial services mirrors this lament. In his case, this was more about preservation of the *stateliness* of the *proper* English language of Shakespeare.[11] Much of this can also be attributed to bias, re-enforced by a Regulatory CoP that, while still related to financial services, has a very distinct filter through which they view the industry they regulate. Further, the policies and culture tend to be more political, for lack of a better word—more in alignment with the governments and legislators they interact with. Interestingly, this culture of formal policy and discussion is much more in line with the culture of many of the standards bodies, likely encouraging the closer relationship and acceptance between those CoPs.

Embracing Data and Standards

Standards, as discussed in previous chapters, have long been integrated into legislation and regulation across industries. Everyone who files taxes can get an idea of the forms and amount of information regulators expect to be reported just for an individual. Throughout a financial lifecycle, regulators seek a window they can look through to make sure all the parts of the system are working properly.

The recent trend since the 2008 Pittsburgh G20 meeting has seen regulators globally shifting their focus toward data. This is not terribly surprising, as practically every industry since the early 2000s has begun to embrace a new world where data is at the forefront of every conversation. Big data, data lakes, data swamps, data wranglers, data whisperers, data stewards, data owners, all became the hot new buzzwords in vogue.

In the rush to this new world of data, however, there remains a distinct lack of expertise. True Chief Data Officers are difficult to come

---

[11] Mencken, H.L. The American Language.

by in the general population, the requirements requiring a new type of renaissance person.[12] And regulators, while they collect massive amounts of information and data points, do not have a secret cadre of data experts lurking somewhere, and are similarly lacking experts, just as the rest of the industry.

Data, however, is complex. Taking aside the complexity of CoPs, the issues of unstructured data, massive data storage across distributed systems, the new and evolving tools for acquiring, storing, curating and analyzing data are daunting to those at the forefront, let alone those new to the space.

It is natural, then, for those unfamiliar to seek out ways to make this change to a data-centric view easier. Standards, a traditional fall back for legislators and regulators, is a much easier transition. Further, as noted earlier, where there are groups of experts that understand that standards do not present a simple silver bullet solution, this information is not promoted and hardly, if ever, leads the discussions when policy makers research standards. The resulting effect is that policy makers are led to the false belief that simply applying standards solve their problems unilaterally.

ESMA has pushed the envelope in running ahead, scissors in hand, mandating standards unilaterally, and ahead of discussions among global regulators within forums like CPMI IOSCO. Like the WTO, ESMA has decidedly come down on the side of only considering ISO standards as *the right* standards. This is not to say ESMA is ignoring the industry. Indeed, it may be the amount they are trying to take on is leading them to look for simple solutions. From October 2015 to October 2020, ESMA published over 100 official Consultations regarding rulemaking, technical requirements, and other items.

Each of these consultations can garner 20 to 100 responses from various industry participants. That amounts to an average of two detailed consultations a month, with a low end of 40 responses to

---

[12] Robinson, R. 2020. "Chief Data Officer as Renaissance Person." *Chief Data Officer Magazine*, https://cdomagazine.tech/cdo_magazine/news_feed/stories/chief-data-officer-as-renaissance-person/article_5664d8ca-e859-11ea-b884-57b62d88c3ec.html (accessed October 2020).

read, consume, and comprehend. ESMA has an estimate staff of 200, which would include support staff for systems, operations, and others that likely would not be responsible for this work. Drinking from this firehose, and trying to distill all of this down, while addressing biases and knowledge gaps is a daunting task. Add in the complications of language differences across CoPs that are responding, and one must wonder if the input is being interpreted as intended.

The Bank of England (BoE) and the Financial Conduct Authority (FCA) also publish consultations, but also tend to take a more interactive and iterative approach to discussions. In January of 2020, the BoE published a lead discussion paper,[13] part one in a multiphase approach in engaging the industry in dialogue. The FCA, as well, noted their data strategy would "review historical data and assess where harm has occurred to learn lessons for the future"[14] in pursuit of data reforms. This included written responses, as well as planned in person meetings (held virtually due to the COVID-19 pandemic). Organizations such as the Transparency Task Force were engaged and held meetings, such as a symposium in September 2020 among global data experts where BoE and FCA leads chaired detailed breakout sessions to discuss issues.

Enforcement Through Mandate

Regulatory policy globally generally comes down to two schools of thought—prescriptive, detailed rules versus principles based regulation. For decades, the U.S. regulators were viewed as heavily prescriptive, whereas the European model, lead generally by the FCA and BoE tended toward the more principles based. Prescriptive regulation aimed at detailing every possible scenario, to close any loopholes that Wall Street firms may try to run through with a large battleship. Principle based regulation tended to leave more nuance—setting the spirit of fair play and intention.

---

[13] Bank of England. 2020. "Transforming Data Collection from the UK Financial Sector". https://bankofengland.co.uk/paper/2020/transforming-data-collection-from-the-uk-financial-sector (accessed October 2020).

[14] Financial Conduct Authority. "Data Strategy." https://fca.org.uk/publications/corporate-documents/data-strategy (accessed October 2020).

Both have positive aspects, and both have drawbacks. Prescriptive regulations set down very clear rules and steps. When "X" happens, "Y" must be done. One drawback to this is the rigidness—it may force significant cost to a firm to comply with certain reporting when the activity they were engaged in was not really the focus of the oversight, and all things being equal, when examined wasn't necessary. Also, it opened up the game of finding loopholes. Given the rigidity of the regulation, if the exploitation of the loophole was sufficiently imaginative, the activity was outside the legal ability for the regulator to oversee it or amend the rule to capture it, even if it fit the *intention* of the rules. Sometimes just renaming a product differently than what it was explicitly called in the rules was enough to get around the rule.

Principle-based regulation, though, can adjust and keep firms more honest in that respect. However, it then comes down to a certain level of subjectivity. In the case of a violation, there would be subjective arguments on both sides that would need to be evaluated on if a rule was broken or not. Also, from the perspective of a firm being regulated, a principle rule may be unclear or genuinely misunderstood. This could introduce costs or risks that, if the rule were clearer, would not be incurred. Firms make calculated risk choices on if they were willing to risk the potential spirit of a principled rule or not in relation to the potential monetary or competitive gain.

Oddly, sometime during the 2000s, as mainland Europe countries, led by Germany, began to assert more authority to counter the FCA's heavy influence, European regulation began to take on a more prescriptive nature. Meanwhile, in the United States, the opposite trend was beginning to be seen, with principle based rules taking hold.

At the same time, standards organizations, like ISO, were pushing to get their standards adopted by financial firms. Changeover to ISO 20022 from ISO 15022 was slow. LEI was being herald as the entity identifier to solve regulator's problems and prevent a repeat of the 2008 debt crisis, but there was little adoption. Regulators, struggling with trying to find ways to report data and trade information they collected in dozens of ways, and sometimes not at all, were counselled that adopting standards would fix those systemic issues. Standards organizations began to press regulators that firms would not voluntarily adopt standards, and therefore, they must be forced to do so for the good of the industry.

Regulations like Markets in Financial Instruments Regulation (MiFIR) and Markets in Financial Instruments Directive (MiFID) began to introduce mandates on using specific standards, both messaging and data identifiers.

This focus on uniformity is, of course, good for the regulators, on the surface. Limited resources in technology systems and people, this would reduce costs while increasing transparency, providing a double benefit for the taxpayers and investors.

And here our story begins to run up against Communities of Practice, and the differences in language and data that has been detailed throughout this book.

This is not to say that regulators made these decisions lightly, or in some cavalier manner. However, there was distinct industry feedback that tried to steer regulators away from the overarching mandates that were put into place. It didn't help that there was no single unified view on what the actual solution should be—exemplifying the diversity of CoPs that existed, and their naturally different practices. In responses by the regulators to the industry, these diverse views were called out as reason why one path must be chosen—as the industry itself did not have agreement. The standard's organizations pronouncements were deemed true—firms simply did not want to adopt standards and would need to be forced to do so.

Viewed in the light of CoPs, this breakdown in communication takes on an interesting perspective. As opposed to firms' stalwart opposition to implementing standards, there is an argument that the standards do not properly align with their community. The fundamental missing observation is that the diversity exists because it necessarily does. The disagreement between industry players is not because they cannot agree, but that they have valid differences that should be recognized. The reality is that the firms have, in fact, implemented standards. Just not the standards that the regulators want them to.

The Anti-Trust Issue

It would be remiss to not mention the issue of regulatory mandates reducing competition, especially through compulsory use of overarching standards. Power and influence have been established previously as reasons why control of language is sought. However, an outcome of this power and influence is the resulting mandated monopoly status conferred upon a standard and any provider of that standard. This translates directly into a monetary incentive to prevent competition, and expand realm of control.

That is not to say that all standards setting activity results in anti-competitive monopoly power. Randi Brown, in a NYU Law contribution notes:

> [W]hile the standard-setting process does frequently have the effect of eliminating competition, competition may not stay down for long. Competing patents can seek standard-essential status even after a standard has been set, and there may also be competing standards addressing a single technological need. For example, 3G, 4G, and LTE are all standards used in providing cell service. Despite the pervasiveness of 3G, 4G still rose up, and LTE therefrom. While the individual patents within these standards were not directly competing to dispel market power in that limited market, the standards themselves were in direct competition, weakening the position of any individual SEP holder on the whole.[15]

However, the nuance here is important to note. Even when a standard is awarded, effectively creating a monopoly owner, there is opportunity for competing standards to emerge, and provide innovation and optionality across the landscape. The problem, however, is when this opportunity is curtailed or prevented, especially through mandates that broadly affect multiple CoPs, even if unintentionally.

Especially in the financial services industry, and, in regards to standards, this is a troubling path that is being pursued. When a single

---

[15] Brown, R. 2018. "Always a Monopoly, Never a Monopolist: Why Antitrust is the Wrong Regulatory Scheme for Protecting Competition in Technical Standards." *NYU Law Moot Court Board Proceeds.* https://proceedings.nyumootcourt. org/2018/04/always-a-monopoly-never-a-monopolist-why-antitrust-is-the-wrong-regulatory-scheme-for-protecting-competition-in-technical-standards/#_ftn8 (accessed October 2020).

standards setting organization is elevated above others, effectively excluding those organizations from producing *competing* standards, this effectively eliminates competition, and introduces significant negative impacts associated with monopoly power. Further, the lack of recognition of multiple CoPs that likely do not speak the language of that singularly ordained standards organization creates serious concerns about disruption to processes, introduction of miscommunication, and a lack of recognition of valid language and data definitions.

Regulators Are Not the Bad Guys (Neither Is Wall Street)

Regulators are doing their job as best they can, in a dynamic and rapidly changing environment; not only across the type of financial activity that takes place, but the structure of firms, the rise of startups in the FinTech space, cryptocurrencies and digital assets, technology running at a pace of change faster than Moore's Law, and the still nascent space that is *data* that lacks significant expertise or understanding.

Further, there does appear to be some awareness that things are more complex than they originally seemed, especially from the BoE, FCA, MAS, and U.S. agencies like the SEC, CFTC and MSRB. The BoE and FCA have authored a few papers around the issues regarding data and the need for interoperability, as well as engaging in expert-invited symposiums, such as the one hosted on September 9, 2020, with the Transparency Task Force. U.S. Agencies have appointed Chief Data Offices in all major agencies, and regulations have begun to speak to principles around open data and choice, rather than strict mandates. MAS hosted a *techsprint*, Project Ubin,[16] on ways to innovate in regulatory reporting and enabling financial market infrastructures, focused on the payments space.

---

[16] Monetary authority of Singapore and TEMASEK. 2020. "Project Ubin's Fifth and Final Phase Highlights Commercial Potential, Paving Way Towards Live Adoption." https://mas.gov.sg/news/media-releases/2020/project-ubin-fifth-and-final-phase-highlights-commercial-potential-paving-way-towards-live-adoption (accessed January 4, 2021).

In the end, regulators, as a community, are struggling with the same issues as the rest of the larger financial services social system. They have on staff their own experts in standards and data that have a decidedly different viewpoint and perspective than the various industry specific CoPs. As regulators tried to learn the language of those they must oversee, there were distinct differences and conflicts. Under the belief that all within financial services spoke the same language, regulators joined with specific standards organizations that pursued a silver bullet solution. The definition of the problem—that not everyone is speaking the same language—was understood. But without taking a linguistic view toward this language problem, a faulty premise led to policies supporting monolingualism and *harmony* as opposed to recognition of multilingualism and interoperability. There are some pockets that appear to have begun to understand this dilemma but there is significant political capital already wrapped up in pursuit of standards that works against any kind of change.

Final Notes on Regulators

As I was finishing up the final edits, I was made aware of a set of new Consultations by IOSCO ("Market Data In The Secondary Equity Markets"),[17] by Her Majesty's Treasury ("Financial Services Future Regulatory Framework Review"),[18] and by the UK Parliament's Treasury Select Committee (Future of Financial Services).[19]

In the IOSCO Consultation, Question 4 asks "How is market data used by different types of investors or different functions of your firm?". I take this as promising—that it, is starting to be understood or acknowledged that data might be used differently by different types of groups or functions. While the question remains unaware of CoPs, it is

---

[17] IOSCO. 2020. "Market Data in the Secondary Equity Markets." iosco.org/library/pubdocs/pdf/IOSCOPD667.pdf (accessed December 2020).

[18] HM Treasury. 2020. "Financial Services Future Regulatory Framework Review Phase II". https://gov.uk/government/consultations/future-regulatory-framework-frf-review-consultation (accessed December 2020).

[19] UK Parliament. 2020. "Future of Financial Services Inquiry Launched." https://committees.parliament.uk/committee/158/treasury-committee/news/132741/future-of-financial-services-inquiry-launched/ (accessed January 4, 2021).

most definitely a welcome step in the right direction. Further, Question 5 asks "What impact does different uses have on the need to access data? How can these impacts be managed or addressed?" Again, showing a heightened awareness of language use being a driving force.

HM Treasury's and the UK Parliament's consultations take aim at the realities of Brexit, as well as the approach differences between the UK and the rest of Europe. In that vein, there would appear to be a desire to return to the more flexible principles-based legislation approach, and the need to remain flexible in light of constantly evolving markets. The willingness to appreciate the complexity that financial services face speaks to a willingness to find new and innovative approaches.

Regulators and legislators in the United States, the United Kingdom, as well as ASEAN markets, such as Singapore, continue to make positive strides toward modernizing markets and looking to the complexity of data. There are pockets that are beginning to understand that data is language, and that financial language is more a conceptualization of a multilinguistic society, not an actual end goal of standardized monolinguistic conformity. This is not to say that this is a universal or broad trend. There is clear indication from other regulators that they plan to *dig in* and dogmatically defend a single standard approach.

CHAPTER 13

Applying Communities of Practice

I promised to provide a functional view of the financial services industry, an understanding of the standards and tools in place today, and the importance of understanding applied linguistics in viewing the issues the industry faces. I hope at this point, these basic pillars have built a foundation for you to examine and analyze the deeper challenges presented by language and language change within Communities of Practice.

To that end, a high level model of the financial industry, through the lens of CoPs was presented, supported by some of the basic principles of linguistics—through Hockett's Design Features, influenced by Saussure, as well as social theory, such as Luhmann's social systems, to the technology traditionally pushed forward to solve problems in today's global environment.

In any social system, there are competing goals that conflict with each other driven by the needs of distinctly different CoPs, even while they all rely on each other to accomplish a higher function such as a functioning global marketplace through overall governance. The required specialization for each part to be able to service the whole naturally creates boundaries between those parts—in culture, process, and therefore language. Language, ever evolving, does so in partial isolation within those parts, re-enforcing multilingualism. This fights against the desire to ease communication and understanding between CoPs, and a natural tendency to blame language differences on willful obstructionism as opposed to the naturally occurring social language construct it is.

Interconnected yet Distinct

As humans, we will group things that are more alike than different together for convenience, especially when comparing groups that have larger general differences. This is easy to see within political and geographic boundaries, such as when we talk about African, European, Middle Eastern, Asian-Pacific, North American, and South American groupings. We do this between industries, as well—manufacturing, technology, retail, financial services, and so on.

Yet, when we examine a *like* group such as European—there is much that differentiates those within the larger European group. When it comes to language, the differences matter to the point where there requires a level of accommodation and fixing at CoP boundaries such that interoperability (e.g., translation) becomes a critical tool to enable understanding and preventing miscommunication.

This can lean toward over engineering, such as drilling down to the individual themselves. Which is why we need to use the guide of what makes a CoP to define the groupings that are appropriate within the context we are pursuing. This subjectivity is problematic to solving issues that face financial services cleanly, especially given the inclination to utilize technology and standards to resolve many of these problems. But ignoring these distinctions or trying to eliminate them outright, is precisely why challenges persist and remain unresolved.

These distinctions are not easily done away with. In looking at what influenced language change in America, Mincken observes that "In particular[,] the generation born in the New World was uncouth and iconoclastic; the only world it knew was a rough world, and the virtues that environment engendered were not those of niceness, but those of enterprise and resourcefulness."[1] Culturally, we could liken this to the front office in financial services. As noted previously, the front office needs to have a leaning toward risk taking, and it is viewed within the financial world as being more rough, less nice, than those colleagues in other areas.

This makes for a distinct culture, apart from their polar opposites in risk and compliance that are decidedly anti-risk taking, where the culture is more methodical and detailed in preventing any type of risk taking. Yet, these two CoPs must find a way to work together to serve the larger social system. Further, this impacts language evolution, as the need is then toward "inventing a vocabulary for the special needs" specific to that CoP, as Minchen would say.

---

[1] Mincken, H.L. 1919. *The American Language*. Knopf.

This goes across the map of CoPs and the processes that span the financial system. Throughout a trade's lifecycle, each CoP has created a specialized vocabulary that enables that CoP to perform its necessary function. It is no trivial matter to simply eliminate or attempt to force change to these through a mono-linguistic approach dictated and enforced by a single CoP, such as regulators or standards groups, upon all others. Ignoring the linguistic reasons why these language differences exist in lieu of attributing them to some conscious intent ignores the reason why distinct CoPs exist in an interconnected system.

Expert Bias

Expert bias plays a significant role in miscommunication between CoPs, as well as supporting false assumptions around standards that I have explored previously. Individual experts within CoPs bear a level of responsibility in perpetuating difficulties in understanding and communication, as much as those experts in other CoPs that are listening. Werner notes that

> Stephen Pinker has a book on linguistics and writing (The Sense of Style)[,] which has a chapter on the problem of expert bias. This goes to the problem with people using jargon and not realizing it. People forget that what has become second-nature to them through constant use is very hard for others to see through.[2]

Our self-awareness, or lack thereof, is re-enforced by our own CoPs in many ways, so that when we do interact with others, we fail to appreciate that the language will be different. For basic concepts, this leads to a problem as what is *second nature* tends to be the hardest to explain sometimes. Try to explain what a cloud is to someone who has never seen one before. As Liberman noted, language change is functionally disadvantaging in hindering communication, especially when dealing with socially dominant groups, such as regulators. But it is a universal fact of language, and the advantage is toward the better cohesion and communication within the CoP.

---

[2] Werner, Thomas, Dean, Linguistics, Carnegie Mellon University (2019). E-mail message to author.

Werner further posits,

> Maybe what is needed in the financial world is for communicators
> to learn some basics of language change and variation so they can
> provide their own accessible paraphrases of what they want to
> say—accessible to the larger community that is, and not only their
> small sub-group. (That said, it is hardly the case the linguists suffer
> from expert bias any less than anyone else.)[3]

We see this bias throughout the different CoPs mentioned in this book, and from the outside, it begins to seem obvious. However, unless one is continuously and actively evaluating their own expert bias when interacting with various CoPs, it is an easy trap to fall back into. The problem being that experts typically view the world through the lens of the CoP they are experts in. Disagreements between meaning lack active fixing or accommodation, especially when pitting two experts from different CoPs against each other.

Each believes their language is the *right* one, and the other's is *wrong*. Which, as I have stated up front, violates a primary principle that there is no right or wrong language.

Communities, Jargon, and Language Change

Expert bias and lack of linguistic expertise are barriers to championing interoperability and multilingualism over monolinguistic efforts. But a key resource in addressing the overall problem is understanding language change within CoPs and evolution of jargon; why it happens, what the impact is, and why when language does change, it does not change universally across a social system like financial services with multiple CoPs.

Jargon, in linguistic terms, is a specialist language that means something to a specific group and is many times unintelligible to those outside. This definition alone is likely to give regulators excuse enough to wish to banish jargon, as it understandably creates opaqueness and a lack of transparency into the very groups they are required to oversee. However, jargon serves purpose.

---

[3] Werner, Thomas, Dean, Linguistics, Carnegie Mellon University (2019). E-mail message to author.

But that is not to say that regulators' fears are unwarranted. Chi Luu, JSTOR's resident linguist, states, "Jargon, as useful as it is in the right contexts, can end up being socially problematic and divisive when it hides and manipulates meanings from those who need to receive the information."[4] They note how English language experts like H.W. Fowler and L.E. Sissman both vilified the use and existence of jargon, precisely because of how it can be used to twist or outright change meaning.

An example in financial services that is easy to refer to is the category of fixed income formally called *junk bonds*. Within the club of traders, *junk* was (and is) a highly lucrative subset of fixed income because (without getting into all the specifics) it is cheap to buy—and therefore, easier to sell to investors. However, there is a reason it was called *junk*—it is cheap to buy because it is highly risky. But that risk aspect was played down in lieu of the higher returns—ten to a hundred times more than traditional, well-qualified fixed income bonds. The term *junk bond* was not used with investors, though. It was the jargon of the front office fixed income world and an open secret up until the market collapse in the late 1980s, primarily due to junk bond investing.

Junk bonds then became a widely known term as media pounced on the jargon and used it as a cudgel to admonish greedy traders. However, that particular asset class never did go away. Nor is there anything particularly wrong with *junk*—as it does serve a role in market economies for funding, especially for those that are well informed about the risks. Today, junk is instead referred to as *High Yield*, focusing more on the returns that are possible, as opposed to the risk aspect, and repair its reputation into a marketable investment. It remains a highly active investment option. They did play into both the Dot-Com bubble and the 2008 mortgage crisis. The Dot-Com bubble was more the fault of speculation on any Internet connected company. The 2008 crisis is notable, as the junk/high yield bonds were packaged and the package was classified as *investment grade*.

But jargon does fill a valid linguistic need unrelated to any kind of deception. It simplifies conversation between two members of the same CoP, enabling the more accurate sharing of information, and eliminating

---

[4] Luu, C. 2018. "The Tangled Web of Jargon." *JSTOR Daily*. https://daily.jstor.org/the-tangled-language-of-jargon/ (accessed October 2020).

misunderstandings, because there is shared acceptance of the jargon-based term. The heavy use of acronyms is one version of jargon. A derivative trader constantly repeating *credit default swap* is not efficient, hence *CDS* becomes the jargon. Yet, *CDS* in back office equity terms is *Central Depository System*. This speaks to not just the utility of jargon, but also the arbitrary nature of language and how jargon is part of language evolution within CoPs.

Another example is also in the credit default world, where referring to *names* infers the *reference entities*, which in turn means the actual bonds and entity that issues the bonds. Traders may call each other and ask "What names do you have?" This jargon is specific to this CoP, as asking an operations person in equity, such a question would sound like non-sense. Similarly, bond traders can tend to speak purely in percentages and years ("Give me two percent at 10 years" meaning to provide them with prices for bonds that have a two percent yield and a 10 year maturity). U.S. Settlement operations use the jargon *DK*, as a shortcut for the jargon *don't know* to reference that they are rejecting a settlement because they do not have instructions to receive a payment or shares. *On the run* is jargon that refers to the most current bond issue, typically treasuries, in a particular group. Stepping into the office of any CoP in financial services, whether the trading desk or back office, to an outsider can be just as unin-telligible as walking the rounds with a doctor in a hospital, regardless of how much *Grey's Anatomy* you have watched.

It should be clear that jargon evolves within CoPs, it is not language that existed. In some cases, the words may have existed, but their mean-ing is changed (as with *names*). Jargon, in most cases, serves a purpose in enabling the better functioning of a CoP, yet has little utility for other CoPs, and actually may be disruptive and cause confusion when the same word has two different meanings across CoPs.

Why Legislating Language (and Standards) Fail

When bringing these issues together in regards to legislation, Professor Kiesling, at the University of Pittsburgh states, "Language is always changing, and it will change in the direction that speakers of a speech community take it (in other words, legislating language change is hard if not impossible)."[5] Yet, the use of broad mandates and standards seek to do just this.

The significant trouble with legislation is that once in place, it is very difficult to change. The same can be said for many standards. This is by design, and a good function, however. What use would any law serve if it was easily changed one day to the next, at the whim of the circumstance? And if a standard is meant to provide a stable foundation to build upon, does it fulfill its function if, depending on manufacturer, it means different things? I know that I rely on my "34-34" size jeans[6] to fit whether they were made in Thailand or Indonesia. Language change not only is inevitable, but it serves a purpose in continually enabling CoPs to adjust to new needs and functions, as well as improve. As I have provided before, CoPs are defined and differentiated by their domain, processes, and culture, and therefore, language change does not happen uniformly across the larger social system of financial services.

The advent of cryptocurrencies and digital tokens, for example, have created a new CoP within financial services that is mostly unintelligible to all those CoPs that already existed. Where there is cross-over and interaction, there is some language adoption and change, such as within back office and custody. But such terms as *hot storage* and *cold storage* (indicating if the cryptocurrency is held connected to a network, or is *offline* disconnected from any network) are not lingua franca universally.

Legislating language, in a prescriptive manner, is akin to legislating that a toddler should stay sitting in one place, and then blaming the parents when they do not. Language is unruly. Language changes because it must, as it learns. More so, if the toddler is forced to stay still, she will not evolve. She will not grow and become a dynamic positive contribution to the larger social system.

And as previously discussed, legislating language is more about power and control, as opposed to producing any kind of real benefit, and has negative consequences for those forced to adopt a non-native language, as

---

[5] Keisling, S. PhD, Linguistics, University of Pittsburgh, via e-mail, August 2019.
[6] Understanding that this is a bit of U.S. based jargon in clothing. Size 34 inch waist, size 34 inch inseam (length).

well as the social system as a whole. At the same time, it fails, as the individual CoP languages will persist, with the simple facade of the *standard* language as a face. And finally, ironically, any imposed *standard* language will change and evolve itself, outpacing any efforts to keep pace within the scripted standard or legislation. Minchen's examples regarding The American Language provide ample representation to that regard.

Communities of Practice in Practice

Application of Communities of Practice promise to provide a new and innovative tool in addressing many of the current issues facing financial services in the area of data, data management, and related concerns in standards and regulation. It is by no means a new silver bullet. The idea is to include the concept of CoPs in the many different processes related to data and language. It is a shift from *harmony* to *interoperability*. It can be as simple as adding a stage in certain efforts that formally ask questions such as "What CoP does this relate to?" Or "What CoP is this data related to?" And "How does the meaning of this data differ between these CoPs? Should it or can it be translated?"

In legislation and regulation, consideration should be taken in clearly defining a CoP where rules will apply—and ensuring that it is properly defined. And in standards, standards organizations and practitioners have to do a better job of formally examining the target CoP, including specific scope in standards, and understand the linguistic issue behind standardization.

CHAPTER 14

The Modest Proposal

In a previous paper, "A linguistics approach to solving financial services standardization,"[1] I present the case that the current approach and methodology for development of standards, and the subsequent application of those standards, was in need of change. Most importantly, the view held by general industry participants, and most significantly the regulatory community, oversimplifies the current environment and oversubscribe the applicability of standards that exist or are under development. To summarize the paper's final findings:

- While a common financial language seems to be a reasonable rallying cry, it presents an oversimplification of what the end goal should be. The real work is in the proper definition and categorization of the various financial languages and dialects that exist.
- The applied linguistics methodologies of translation and interoperability should be employed between what already exists; they should not just be an attempt at *normalized standardization* across all domain geographies. Shared language does not translate to shared meaning.
- Ontologies can become big and unwieldy if they try to take on too much. However, they are a critical tool in creating the adapters for translation. Multiple ontologies must exist; no

---

[1] Robinson, R.C. 2012 "Project Ubin's Fifth and Final Phase Highlights Commercial Potential, Paving Way Towards Live Adoption." *Journal of Financial Market Infrastructures* 7, no. 2, December 2018.
https://risk.net/journal-of-financial-market-infrastructures/6119456/a-linguistics-approach-to-solving-financial-services-standardization (accessed January 4, 2021).

single ontology (i.e., FIBO) can address the full universe of financial languages alone.

- Ontologies do not replace existing standards and languages. It needs to be realized that any existing *legacy* will continue to persist and needs to be supported.

Data is the stored foundation of financial language. However, due to varying factors, different CoPs within financial services define similar seeming data differently. Not only is the language different, but many times, the meaning is also different. Financial language and the data it utilizes is meant, as any language, to support a cooperative activity. How broadly or narrow that cooperative activity is defined affects how specifically any data used in that activity can be defined. In this way, a cooperative activity can be aligned with what we term context.

From the aforementioned, I propose that any cooperative activity can be bound by the elements that create the context within a specific community; the parties involved, and the specific role they are playing, the perspective of the party defining the data, how the data was sourced/ created, and intention(s) for use. How broadly or narrow the context and CoP is defined will affect the usability of data; data used in a broad context will, in most cases, be unusable for reuse or application in a more narrow subset context for specific tasks within individual CoPs. In the same way, specific data from different contexts may not *survive* when used in a broader context and/or aggregated with similar data from different contexts, even within a CoP.

I stated earlier that a trade is not always a trade. *Trade* in a Chompskyan universal grammar aspect is fairly consistent—it is something exchanged for something else between parties. However, this meaning lacks the specificity that different CoPs attach to it, that has a real impact on processes and pro-cedures, as well as interactions between CoPs. It ignores the evolution the term has gone through while in use in those different CoPs, leveraging the language for their specific needs. Are we talking executions, or settlements? What about allocations? Are we discussing *trade* as it related to GDP (Gross Domestic Product)? When viewing liquidity, you wouldn't use trade settle-ments, but instead trade executions; but only executions across the markets that are relevant to calculating liquidity for a specific purpose. It's a con-stantly unpeeling onion, which is why using a singular standard definition for these concepts without context is potentially more dangerous than using no standards at all. Further, the different CoPs that are using the term *trade* differently, store their data within that specific context. So, a *trade* as an object within one CoP, when compared to a *trade* stored as an object within a different CoP are like comparing apples to oranges. The associated data may be completely different, from pricing calculations, to the data needed to identify the various parties and accounts involved.

So, how do we start to create a framework to traverse this interconnected web of overly broad versus overly specific data definitions (semantics specific to a purpose) and contexts? How do we improve the system that exists without looking to completely overhaul and disrupt everything?

Education

The first step in this modest proposal is the one I am taking here with this book. Simply identifying the problem and trying to define it in a way that is accessible and usable. Education and constructive discourse about the themes around CoPs presented in this book are needed, across industry organizations, standards organizations, and regulators. A healthy debate on the conclusions, their merits and implications can only help to better inform the conversation moving forward.

But this cannot be done in isolation, disconnected from industry, regulatory, and standards conversations. Because a wide range of expertise must be included. But even more important, a larger population representing the different CoP experts must be brought into the conversation.

This is, in essence, a call to shift behaviors from a blame behavior to one that tries to first understand different perspectives. It is about collaboration and agreeing that it is possible for two things to be right, instead of one answer right and one answer wrong. It is about understanding that multiple answers can be right at the same time, and the challenge is in how to interoperate while preserving that perspective.

Inclusion of Applied Linguistics

Technology has led the charge into data. And even as we pull business experts into the data conversation, whether it be through formal data governance with roles like stewards, or informally through business ownership of data assets, there is a fundamental skill regarding linguistics that is lacking. For all the advances in the data realm, we essentially can still be arguing over Oracle versus Sybase, but instead distributed storage or centralized, NoSQL or SQL, knowledge graphs versus ontologies.

From a technology angle, we are still focused around storage and retrieval, with a veneer of classification to make categorization easier. But identification and classification and relationships in data are purely focused on how that data should be captured and stored, as opposed to understanding the data in a more advanced way. There is an assumption that data fits the context for the application that is being built, and if you can grab more data, the machine can analyze it and figure out its relevance.

Even more dangerously, it is assumed that we all speak the same language. Nor is it exclusive to financial services, but in a significant number of global arenas, particularly when we use the English language. I have given a very simplistic view of CoPs as a basic foundation. But there remains the additional complexities of communicating and translating across human languages

There is a need for the subjective expertise of the applied linguist within financial services, not to mention many other industries. The thousands of years of study in linguistics is one of the oldest areas of study in the world. Technology in ML, AI, and NLP steal from linguistics but give it only a passing nod in many cases, resulting in the ignoring of bias, CoP differentiation, and context.

Werner suggested some early steps may be focused on "find[ing] (short) excerpts from financial writing or speaking and show where jargon is being used and precisely why this jargon impedes understanding, this would be the basis for concrete proposals for addressing the problem."[2] We have offered some examples through jargon, and in discussion of the arbitrariness principle. This can form a basis for organizations to focus more on interoperability and identifying where translation between CoPs and CoP specifically defined standards are needed and need to be maintained.

---

[2] Werner, Thomas, Dean, Linguistics, Carnegie Mellon University (2019). E-mail message to author.

Coordination

I do not hold any illusions that the task before the financial services community is an easy one in regards to being able to integrate the concepts of CoPs and applied linguistics. But I would not be writing this book if I did not believe it is critical, and I have received nothing but support and agreement from a broad group of colleagues—new and old—with whom I continue to consult. To enable this, there remains the need for a global financial services standards organization, as proposed by Houstoun et al. (2015, p. 71), that brings together the different standards organizations active in the industry, regulators, and the industry as a whole under a single collaborative guiding body, ironically the mission of ISO's predecessor. An independent best practices organization that has no ties to lobbying and is a vendor-neutral forum, such as ISITC (ISITC.org), could possibly be a good home for this.

Establishment of some forum, specific to financial services, that can help maintain and grow a map of the CoPs that exist, how they relate to each other and interact is dearly needed. This can't be authoritative, but informative for when applying standards or policies. It needs to evolve, like language does, to capture and help catalogue the reality and complexity of the CoPs that exist within financial services. Simple recognition that these CoPs exist can go a long way.

There is a slight naiveté to this, of course. As discussed multiple times, control of language is a source of power. And essentially, this aspect is looking for organizations to limit and possibly give up some of the perceived power they wield. This translates into money and influence. But the hope here is that organizations, and individuals, see the larger value that can be built by focusing on interoperability, rather than dominance, over the long run. Understanding, and then actively managing the evolution of language across CoPs in a collaborative way holds massive potential for creating transparency, reducing risks, reducing costs, and creating new value across the industry.

Leadership From Authorities

Regulatory regimes can most effectively benefit the industry by attempting to resolve the legal barriers that create friction, rather than by mandating the use of specific standards across broad universes. Take, for instance, TARGET2-Securities, which has removed clearing regime barriers in Europe as opposed to legislating standards in business process language. There has been good work by CPMI-IOSCO, the CFTC, FCA, and others in holding open forums to discuss issues with the industry. Yet, it seems these efforts are in the minority, and it is difficult to properly capture and implement the many voices of the industry rationally without a better roadmap.

I have raised a number of concerns around current trends in policies and standards that, when viewed through the lens of CoPs, should highlight how authorities can better approach the industry. Adversarial relationships grow from lack of understanding that creates mistrust through misunderstanding. Warranted, there are some specific cases where desire for transparency and fairness has the potential to impact business models and profitability, which will create conflict between industry and authorities. But even in these cases, a better understanding of the impact of CoPs, and how they interact could perhaps lead to alternatives that serve as better compromises.

The goals of transparency and fairness are only achieved through active engagement and mutual understanding and acceptance. Authorities should embrace this approach, in pursuit of their primary mission for protection of global and national markets.

Final Thoughts

I hope some of what I have said here resonates. And if it does, get involved. I am sure there will be resistance, and some outright objections to things I have stated. But I am not afraid of controversy. The first thing I would ask is that if as a reader, you take objection, first think again back to what CoPs are all about, as that really is the main purpose of this book. If then there still are issues, that is what constructive conversation is for. This is not a 'you must do things this way' instruction guide, but a 'there are other perspectives' introduction to application of linguistics.

In recap, I looked to provide an overview of financial services, how standards are applied, and how the lens of applied linguistics and CoPs could improve what we do, and solve some long-standing problems. Data is the expression of language in financial services (and other industries).

And language changes and evolves over time, in response to the needs of a CoP—without any corresponding change in the language of other CoPs within the same social system. This is not right or wrong, and is not something that can be controlled or prevented through standards or legislation.

Technology can provide some tools, but to solve communication issues that involve language, we need to look to language experts— specifically applied linguistics that focuses on solving problems regarding language interaction. In doing so, we also need to shift our focus and perception of what should be the solutions we employ—embracing CoP specific standards, and focusing work on interoperability and recognition, in order to better aid accommodation and fixing between CoPs. I do not discount the power and utility of ontology tools, data scientists' approaches to semantics, things like RDF/OWL, SHACL, and so forth. But a tool as powerful as XML didn't actually solve anything. It is how technology is applied, and how those tools are directed and used that solves issues. This is where we need to figure out how to insert CoP's into the methodologies and discussions involving ontologies, semantics, and context. It introduces a complicating factor, for certain, but one that needs to be addressed. This will result in better understanding, less conflict, more transparency, better data, and more efficient markets. But only with active education and inclusion of applied linguistics, with coordination across the industry, supported by leadership from global authorities can this become an established ongoing exercise that may finally realize hopes from 20 years ago started by the likes of Giovaninni and the G30.

Appendix A

Standard And/Or Project Under The Direct Responsibility OF ISO/TC 68/SC 9 Secretariat (27)

ISO 1004-1:2013
Information processing — Magnetic ink character recognition — Part 1: Print specifications for E13B

ISO 1004-2:2013
Information processing — Magnetic ink character recognition — Part 2: Print specifications for CMC7

ISO 8532:1995
Securities — Format for transmission of certificate numbers

ISO 8583-1:2003
Financial transaction card originated messages — Interchange message specifications — Part 1: Messages, data elements and code values

ISO 8583-2:1998
Financial transaction card originated messages — Interchange message specifications — Part 2: Application and registration procedures for Institution Identification Codes (IIC)

ISO 8583-3:2003
Financial transaction card originated messages — Interchange message specifications — Part 3: Maintenance procedures for messages, data elements and code values

ISO 9144:1991
Securities — Optical character recognition line — Position and structure

ISO 11649:2009
Financial services — Core banking — Structured creditor reference to remittance information

ISO 12812-1:2017
Core banking — Mobile financial services — Part 1: General framework

ISO/TS 12812-2:2017
Core banking — Mobile financial services — Part 2: Security and data protection for mobile financial services

ISO/TS 12812-3:2017
Core banking — Mobile financial services — Part 3: Financial application lifecycle management

ISO/TS 12812-4:2017
Core banking — Mobile financial services — Part 4: Mobile payments-to-persons

ISO/TS 12812-5:2017
Core banking — Mobile financial services — Part 5: Mobile payments to businesses

ISO 15022-1:1999
Securities — Scheme for messages (Data Field Dictionary) — Part 1: Data field and message design rules and guidelines

ISO 15022-1:1999/COR 1:1999
Securities — Scheme for messages (Data Field Dictionary) — Part 1: Data field and message design rules and guidelines — Technical Corrigendum 1:.

ISO 15022-2:1999
Securities — Scheme for messages (Data Field Dictionary) — Part 2: Maintenance of the Data Field Dictionary and Catalogue of Messages

ISO 15022-2:1999/COR 1:1999
Securities — Scheme for messages (Data Field Dictionary) — Part 2: Maintenance of the Data Field Dictionary and Catalogue of Messages — Technical Corrigendum 1:.

ISO 18245:2003
Retail financial services — Merchant category codes

ISO 20022-1:2013
Financial services — Universal financial industry message scheme — Part 1: Metamodel

ISO 20022-2:2013
Financial services — Universal financial industry message scheme — Part 2: UML profile

ISO 20022-3:2013
Financial services — Universal financial industry message scheme — Part 3: Modelling

ISO 20022-4:2013
Financial services — Universal financial industry message scheme — Part 4: XML Schema generation

ISO 20022-5:2013
Financial services — Universal financial industry message scheme — Part 5: Reverse engineering

ISO 20022-6:2013
Financial services — Universal financial industry message scheme — Part 6: Message transport characteristics

ISO 20022-7:2013
Financial services — Universal financial industry message scheme — Part 7: Registration

ISO 20022-8:2013

Financial services — Universal financial industry message scheme — Part 8: ASN.1 generation

ISO 22307:2008

Financial services — Privacy impact assessment

Under SC2:

Standard And/Or Project Under the Direct Responsibility Of Iso/Tc 68/ Sc 2 Secretariat (16)

ISO 9564-1:2017

Financial services — Personal Identification Number (PIN) management and security — Part 1: Basic principles and requirements for PINs in card-based systems

ISO 9564-2:2014

Financial services — Personal Identification Number (PIN) management and security — Part 2: Approved algorithms for PIN encipherment

ISO 9564-4:2016

Financial services — Personal Identification Number (PIN) management and security — Part 4: Requirements for PIN handling in eCommerce for Payment Transactions

ISO 11568-1:2005

Banking — Key management (retail) — Part 1: Principles

ISO 11568-2:2012

Financial services — Key management (retail) — Part 2: Symmetric ciphers, their key management and life cycle

ISO 11568-4:2007

Banking—Keymanagement(retail)—Part4:Asymmetriccryptosystems— Key management and life cycle

ISO 13491-1:2016

Financial services — Secure cryptographic devices (retail) — Part 1: Concepts, requirements and evaluation methods

ISO 13491-2:2017

Financial services — Secure cryptographic devices (retail) — Part 2: Security compliance checklists for devices used in financial transactions

ISO 13492:2019

Financial services — Key-management-related data element — Application and usage of ISO 8583-1 data elements for encryption

ISO/TR 14742:2010

Financial services — Recommendations on cryptographic algorithms and their use

ISO 16609:2012

Financial services — Requirements for message authentication using symmetric techniques

ISO/TR 19038:2005

Banking and related financial services — Triple DEA — Modes of operation — Implementation guidelines

ISO 19092:2008

Financial services — Biometrics — Security framework

ISO 20038:2017

Banking and related financial services — Key wrap using AES

ISO 21188:2018

Public key infrastructure for financial services — Practices and policy framework

ISO/TR 21941:2017

Financial services — Third-party payment service providers

Table A.1 Standards organizations and related industry associations

Organization	Purpose/Type	Relevant Standards	Membership Model	Funding	Best at addressing
ISO	International Standards/multiple industries	Owned by TC68: 3166 – Country Codes 17442 – LEI 20022 – message scheme 6166 – ISIN 10383 – MIC 10962 – CFI 18774 – FISN 15022 – Data field dictionary 4217 – Currencies 9362 – BIC 13616 – IBAN	Closed/restricted	Membership fees and IP on created standards. Formed as a Non-Governmental Organization.	Global/cross-country collaboration needed. Single use/single perspective. Broad stroke frameworks. Global adoption of existing standards created by liaisons and others.
W3C	International Web standards		Open membership, individuals by invite	Tiered membership fees. Non-incorporated consortium.	Technical web-related needs
FIX	Standards for trading functions	FIXML	Open, but focused on participants and vendors in the trading/execution process	Tiered membership fees. Non-profit community.	Trading/execution focused issues. Typically inter-party messaging globally.

(Continued)

Table A.1 (Continued)

Organization	Purpose/Type	Relevant Standards	Membership Model	Funding	Best at addressing
OMG	International technology standards	UML, CORBA, FIBO, FIGI	Open membership	Tiered membership fees. Not-for-profit consortium	Enterprise-level technical standards focused on integration / interoperability
ISDA / FpML	Communication of swaps ('OTC Derivatives') related information and flows	FpML	Membership based on firm fitting role of a dealer, service provider, or end-user. Application evaluated by board for fit.	Membership fees. Not-for-Profit Corporation	Firms focused in the derivatives marketplace, especially within 'OTC' type derivatives, interparty communication.
ANSI, BSI (and other 'national' standards bodies)	Nationally-focused standards or new broad-based local standards that may have global applicability (for future ISO submission)	CUSIP (ANSI)	Various models depending on jurisdiction and organization structure	Typically membership fees. Various incorporations.	National issues, and important for collecting experts that can represent national interests at global ISO representation
XBRL	XML business information exchange	XBRL	Open	Dues, education, certifications	Reporting accounting, non-structured information (founded by American Institute of CPA's)

Related Organizations/Support Organizations in Standards Work (1 of 2)				
Organization	Purpose/Type	Membership Model	Funding	Best at addressing
SWIFT	International Bank consortium	Restricted on firm type and size. User forums open based on individual expertise.	Not-for-profit, plus guarantee fund. (User forums are free of charge.)	Originally for payments, but expanded into post-trade messaging for custodians and clients and other service providers. Inter-party messaging globally. Registration Authority for MIC, BIC, IBAN, 15022/20022 Hosts MyStandards.swift.com Runs Securities Evaluation Groups for ISO15022/ISO20022 (based on ISO policy/procedure for maintenance of standards)
Bloomberg (Open Symbology)	Through OpenFIGI, Registration Authority for the OMG FIGI standard	N/A; open data standard. Currently setting up independent Advisory Board composed of industry experts	Private funding through Bloomberg L.P.	Financial instrument identification, data quality, management and governance Hosts www.OpenFIGI.com
Markit	Operates RED code for Credit Default Swaps identification	N/A, private firm	Commercial	Credit Default Swaps

(Continued)

Related Organizations/Support Organizations in Standards Work (1 of 2)				
Organization	Purpose/Type	Membership Model	Funding	Best at addressing
ANNA (Association of National Numbering Agencies)	Trade association for promoting interests of national numbering agencies	Limited to firms self-designated as a 'national numbering agency' and review/ accepted by ANNA board	unknown	Currently Registration Authority for ISO6166
SIX Group	Market Data provider	Private firm	Commercial	RA for 4217
SMPG / NMPG	Securities Market Practice Group/National Market Practice Groups	Open	SWIFT, other	Mixture of ISO and related support organizations that attempt to harmonize best practices globally
EDM Council	Promoting good Data Management practices (U.S., some UK)	Open membership	Membership fees, conferences, educational sessions	Addressing data standards and issues. Coordinating across multiple other organizations/efforts regarding data. On and off support of OMG FIBO efforts. Some lobbying efforts
ISITC	International Financial Services best practices (global firms and representation, U.S. based, UK arm)	Open; firm and individual. Vendor-neutral (no specific vendor/solution endorsement allowed)	Membership, yearly conference. Non-profit	Utilizing existing standards, addressing gaps and setting de facto practices
Data Coalition	U.S. – focused open data lobbying group	Open membership	Membership fees, conferences. Non-profit.	Lobbying for open data regulations in government and related legislation

Related Organizations/Support Organizations in Standards Work (cont.)				
Organization	Purpose/Type	Membership Model	Funding	Best at addressing
SIFMA (US), AFME (EU), ASIFMA(Asia), GFMA (global)	Related securities industry organizations	Firm and individual	Tiered funding model	Multiple functions including; lobbying, committees addressing specific issues, educational seminars, professional networking, subject matter sharing
Investment Association (UK)	Represents UK Investment Managers	Firm (limited to UK Investment Managers)	Member dues	Multiple functions including; lobbying, committees addressing specific issues, educational seminars, professional networking, subject matter sharing
BVI (Germany)	German Investment Funds Association	Firm (limited)	Dues	Multiple functions including; lobbying, committees addressing specific issues, educational seminars
FESE	Federation of European Securities Exchanges (EU)	Firm (limited)	Dues	Represents interests of the exchanges within the EU, in regards to lobbying and shared issues
ABA (US)	American Bankers Association	Firm (limited)	Dues, licensing fees from standards (CUSIP)	Represents the interests of American banks; focus on small and mid-tier banks
SIIA / FISD	Financial & Information Services Association (U.S. based, but global – hold events in Europe, Asia, South American regularly)	Firm (open)	Dues, certification courses, events	Examines technical and data related issues for Financial Services, best practice recommendations, mostly tech firm/ vendor-driven
FIA	Futures industry association	Firm	Dues, conferences	Lobbying, support, education and forums for futures markets related needs

Table A.2 Various firm roles

Role	Primary Relationship	Secondary relationship	Functional role	Notes	Example (Generic/Global Broker Specific)
Client	Asset Manager/ Global Custodian		The individual or firm looking to invest their own assets in a marketplace		Could be an independent Fund, individual, or business with investible assets. A client may direct their Manager actively (so the Manager is simply an *order taker*) or expect the Manager to conform to specific targets/SLA's around performance.
Asset / Investment Manager	Client		The manager is an agent hired by the client to manage investment of its assets	the client may manage its own assets and portfolio	A firm like Fidelity manages most of its own Funds. A firm like Vanguard does both—manages their own funds, but also provides services to other funds.
Introducing Broker	Client/Manager		Manage relationships with clients/managers, provide information and sales, and forward client orders on to Execution brokers to execute on sales made		An introducing broker may go to an executing trader in their own firm (riskless principal/ facilitation/principal trading), or an external broker with access to the required marketplace (agency)

U.S.-based Sales may work directly with a Local (U.S.-based) Int'l Trader (riskless principal, facilitation, principal), or elect to go to a Global Trader in the direct marketplace (agency; at a related firm based in the specific market), or even another external broker (agency; so a Barclay's sales trader in the United States going to a Goldman executing broker) |

	Client/Manager	Introducing broker			
Executing Broker	executing broker		The broker or dealer that finalizes an order on behalf of the client (riskless principal, facilitation, principal) or on behalf of the introducing broker (agency)	An executing broker may also be the introducing broker, although Sales (introducing) and Trading (execution) roles must be separate	An executing broker may be a member on one or more exchanges and execute on their own behalf. For markets where they are not members, they must use an agent in the marketplace to perform the execution on the exchange on their behalf A broker in the United States is a member of NYSE and Nasdaq (for example, Deutsche Bank Securities AG, U.S.). They (DB Securities AG) are not a member of the LSE. That broker's UK arm (i.e., Deutsche Bank London) is a member of the LSE, but not a member of the NYSE
Executing Agent		Local Exchange	The broker or dealer that has membership on a specific exchange and can execute orders on that exchange	An executing agent may be the executing broker	An executing agent has direct membership on a particular exchange/marketplace and is able to effect orders in that exchange/marketplace As previously shown, noted that a Local broker in one market must use an agent for any Int'l orders that are outside of their home market. For example, a U.S. broker would utilize a UK broker (or an UK arm of their firm) for LSE executions. In Brazil, for example, local market regulations require Local utilization of a Brazilian broker.

(Continued)

Table A.2 (Continued)

Role	Primary Relationship	Secondary relationship	Functional role	Notes	Example (Generic/Global Broker Specific)
Settlement Broker	Executing agent	Executing broker	The institution that settles orders executing on the exchange on behalf of the executing agent	A settlement broker may be the executing agent (and executing broker)	A settlement broker is registered as a valid clearing entity for the local exchange/marketplace. The settlement broker settles executions performed on the exchange by the execution agent. The settlement may be on a net basis against the brokers on the other side, or versus a Central Counterparty (CCP). The settlement broker may be the executing broker it is performing services on behalf of.
					In the United States, a U.S. Broker is a member of NSCC for the purposes of clearing trades executing on NYSE/Nasdaq. This U.S. broker will be the settlement agent for executions they performed for their clients (i.e., Executing brokers) in the U.S., as well as for executions they performed as Execution Agent for other brokers. In the UK, the UK broker arm is a member of CREST for the purpose of settling executions performed on the LSE. They will settle executions performed on their own behalf, as well as for executions performed for the U.S. arm of the brokerage as introducing broker (agency) or for the U.S. broker as executing broker (riskless principal, facilitation, principal)

Term	Definition	Notes	Description
Clearing/ Regional Custodian Broker	The institution that manages the holding and transfer of securities on behalf of the executing broker (to/from the client and to/from the settlement broker)	A clearing broker may be the executing broker and/or the settlement broker	The clearing broker will act on behalf of the executing broker to coordinate the receiver of shares executed in the market (on exchange by the execution agent) from the settlement broker, who has received the shares from the exchange (or CCP). Additionally, the clearing broker will manage the onward delivery of those shares on behalf of the executing broker, to the client and/or manager. They will manage the segregation of the executing broker's positions from others
Executing broker			In the United States, most large brokers act as their own clearing broker for assets transacted within the U.S. market. It also will manage the segregation and transfer of U.S. assets purchased by non-U.S. clients through any Global related entity (regardless of agency or principal trading status). Similarly, the Global entity will manage the non-U.S. assets purchased/sold by their U.S.-based entity on behalf of the U.S. based clients

(Continued)

Table A.2 (Continued)

Role	Primary Relationship	Secondary relationship	Functional role	Notes	Example (Generic/Global Broker Specific)
Local Agent	Clearing broker/ Regional Custody broker		The institution that has membership in the local depository and can affect the movement of shares on behalf of the clearing broker		The local agent will take instructions from the clearing broker to receive shares from the settlement broker through the local depository system the local agent is a member of. Additionally, they will take instruction from the clearing broker to onward deliver shares through the depository to the Client's sub-custodian. In the United States, the U.S. based broker (ie. DB Sec AG) is typically a member of DTCC, the local depository. In the UK, the UK based entity (i.e., DB Sec London) is a member of CREST, the local UK depository. Where Global (a DB Sec London) has European assets that are Depositories outside of CREST (France Sicovam, Italy Monti Titoli, etc.), Global contracts with a Local Agent that has a depository relationship in that marketplace (Citibank France, Citibank Italy). Except in markets that do not allow omnibus, the Local Agent (Citibank) makes no knowledge of the (underlying beneficiary) client and only knows the assets belong to Global (DB Sec London). The UK Broker as custodian must ensure to segregate shares properly. This is currently under review as clients must have separate account at agent in most markets (So, in Spain, a distinct account must exist for every beneficiary, so DB Sec London couldn't maintain accounting records only internally to segregate accounts, but must physically have accounts established at their Local Agent as well.

Global Custodian	Client	Manager	The institution that acts as custodial agent on behalf of the client, and the Manager as the client's agent	A Fund, individual, business or other kind of client typically is required to have a "bank account" or Custodian who safekeeps their assets. The Global Custodian is able to centralize all activity done internationally by a client, and provide additional services (such as securities lending facilities, overdraft/cash management services, and so forth). The Custodian is the primary accounting and bookkeeping agent for the beneficiary of the assets. This basic service is distinctly separate from other businesses a "custodian bank" may now be involved with (such as Investment Management Outsourcing).

(Continued)

Table A.2 (*Continued*)

Role	Primary Relationship	Secondary relationship	Functional role	Notes	Example (Generic/Global Broker Specific)
Sub Custodian	Global Custodian		The institution that has membership in the local depository and can affect the movement of shares on behalf of the global custodian	The sub custodian may be the Global Custodian	A sub-custodian is a local banking institution akin to the Local Agent. A sub custodian is hired by a Global Custodian to act as its local agent in a marketplace outside of the firm's primary domicile. The sub custodian may be a related arm of the global custodian. For example. The Bank of New York, U.S., may use BNYM Brussels, to act as its local agent in Belgium. Also, BNYM NY U.S. is its own local agent in the U.S. market. BNYM NY U.S. may hire Bank Itau in Brazil to act as their local agent in Brazil (because either BNYM has no arm in Brazil, or they find that Bank Itau provides better services specific to the client's needs)

Exchange	Exchange members (Executing Agents)	"Exchange" is a type of "venue".	A marketplace in which securities, commodities, derivatives and other financial instruments are traded. The core function of an exchange is to ensure fair and orderly trading, as well as efficient dissemination of price information for any securities trading on that exchange. Exchanges give companies, governments and other groups a platform to sell securities to the investing public.
Depository	Depository members (Local Agents and Sub Custodians)		Central security depositories allow brokers and other financial companies to deposit securities where book entry and other services can be performed, like clearance, settlement and securities borrowing and lending, DTCC, CREST, Deutsche Bourse are examples of Depositories. Euroclear is an "International Central Securities Depository"—offering "depository" like services by using a network of sub-custodian like relationships for access to 'local' CSD's globally

References

"29 CFR § 2510.3-21—Definition of 'Fiduciary.'" 2020. *Cornell Law School, Legal Information Institute.* https://law.cornell.edu/cfr/text/29/2510.3-21 (accessed January 4, 2021).

"Ludwig Wittgenstein." *Stanford Encyclopedia of Philosophy.* https://plato.stanford.edu/entries/wittgenstein/ (accessed January 4, 2021).

"Progress through Collaboration: A New Investment Roadmap." *International Swaps and Derivatives Association.* https://isda.org/a/RciDE/press101210.pdf (accessed January 2021).

2010. "Investment Roadmap." *Fix Trading Community.* https://fixtrading.org/standards/other-standards/investment-roadmap/ (accessed January 4, 2021).

Ali, R.D., A.G. Haldane, and P. Nahai-Williamson. 2012. *Building a Global Legal Entity Framework.*

Asia Pacific Economic Consortium. "Founding and Structure." *APEC Business Advisory Council.* https://www2.abaconline.org//page-content/2521/content (accessed January 4, 2021) https://x9.org/missions-and-objectives/ (accessed August 2020).

Borad, S.B. n.d. "Bonds and their Types." *Sources of Finance.* https://efinancemanagement.com/sources-of-finance/bonds-and-their-types (accessed June 2020).

Brace, E. "Referring to Wittgenstein's Later Theory of Meaning." https://theliteracybug.com/meaning-form (accessed May 2020).

Bruffee, K.A. 1986. "Social Construction, Language, and the Authority of Knowledge: A Bibliographical Essay." *College English* 48, no. 8, 773–790. doi:10.2307/376723. https://jstor.org/stable/376723 (accessed October 7, 2020).

BSI. 2021. "Our purpose, Mission, and Vision." https://bsigroup.com/en-US/about-bsi/inspiring-trust-for-a-more-resilient-world/ (accessed January 4, 2021).

BSI. 2021. "What is a Standard?" *Understand Standards and Schemes for Certification, Information About Standards.*

Chisholm, M., and A. Milne. 2013. "The Prospects for Common Language in Wholesale Financial Services." Working Paper 2012-005, Swift Institute. URL: https://bit.ly/2NU7d1K (accessed August 2019).

Chisolm, A.M. 2010. *Derivatives Demystified*, 2nd ed. New York, NY: Wiley Finance.

Cook, G. 2003. "The "Design Features" of Language." *Applied Linguistics*. Oxford, Oxford University Press.

Diglossia and Power: Language Policies and Practices in 19th Century Habsburg Empire, edited by Rosita Rindler Schjerve.

Dor, D. 2011. "Language as a Social Construct." (video). https://ynetnews.com/articles/0,7340,L-4059809,00.html

Dr. Schestowitz, R. 2008. "ISO and Microsoft: The Corruption Resumes" http://techrights.org/2008/07/11/ooxml-corruption-resumes/ (accessed July 2020).

Dr. Schestowitz, R. 2009. "Company that Attacks ODF Gains More Control of ODF (and why Open Source Should be Careful, Too)." http://techrights.org/2009/10/02/odf-tc-hijack/ (accessed July 2020).

Dr. Schestowitz, R. 2009. "ISO Urged to Invalidate OOXML as Microsoft's Role Gets Shown; More Smears of ODF Come from Microsoft." http://techrights.org/2009/10/17/iso-allies-bashing-odf/ (accessed July 2020).

Duan, M. 2012. "On the Arbitrary Nature of Linguistic Sign." *Theory and Practice in Language Studies* 2, no. 1, pp. 54–59.

Edward, F. n.d. "What is 'Correct' Language?" https://linguisticsociety.org/resource/what-correct-language (accessed February 2020).

European Central Bank. 2009. "Settling Without Borders." https://ecb.europa.eu/pub/pdf/other/settlingwithoutborders_t2sbrochure112009en.pdf (accessed April 2020).

European Commission. 2016. "FISMA: financial data standardization 2016.15." Report, European Commission. https://bit.ly/2yNQuY9 (accessed August 2019).

European Commission. 2017. "Fitness Check on Supervisory Reporting. Consultation Document, European Commission." https://bit.ly/2J6R73N (accessed August 2019).

European Commission. 2017. "Summary Report of the Public Consultation on the Fitness Check on Supervisory Reporting having Taken Place from December 1, 2017 to March 14, 2018." https://ec.europa.eu/info/sites/info/files/2017-supervisory-reporting-requirements-summary-report_en.pdf (accessed October 2020).

European Committee for Standardization. 2021. "What is a Standard?" *European Committee for Standardization, Standards Development*. https://cen.eu/work/ENdev/whatisEN/Pages/default.aspx (accessed January 4, 2021).

FINRA. n.d. "Type of Bonds." https://finra.org/investors/learn-to-invest/types-investments/bonds/types-of-bonds (accessed June 2020).

FIX trading community. n.d. "Mission Statement." https://fixtrading.org/mission-statement/ (accessed January 4, 2021).

Fortune, S. 2004. "A Brief History of Databases." http://avant.org/project/history-of-databases/ (accessed July 2020).

G20. 2021. "About the G20." https://g20.org/en/about/Pages/default.aspx (accessed January 4, 2021). https://group30.org/about (accessed August 2020).

G30 Working Group. 2003. "Global Clearing and Settlement: A Plan of Action." Report, G30. URL: https://bit.ly/2P5accf (accessed August 2019).

Gleeson, B., and M. Rozo. 2013. "The Silo Mentality: How to Break Down the Barriers." *Forbes.* https://forbes.com/sites/brentgleeson/2013/10/02/the-silo-mentality-how-to-break-down-the-barriers/#554ede888c7e (accessed March 2020).

Groenfeldt, T. 2015. "Silos Can Be Costly In Banks." *Forbes.* https://forbes.com/sites/tomgroenfeldt/2015/12/28/silos-can-be-costly-in-banks/#700ee642356f (accessed March 2020).

Haldane, A.G. 2012. "Towards a Common Financial Language. Speech, Securities Industry and Financial Markets Association (SIFMA) Symposium, New York, March 14." Bank for International Settlements. URL: www.bis.org/review/r120315g.pdf (accessed August 2019).

Hall, S.W. 2011. *Mapping Applied Linguistic.* New York, NY: Routledge.

Hanson, R.H. 2016. "Letter to City of Burton, MI." https://static1.squarespace.com/static/56748c1d25981d39eaa27bed/t/5a3157b853450a1a416f8478/1513183160422/DIPRA+letter+to+Mayor+Zelenko.pdf (accessed July 2020).

Harris, L. 2002. *Trading and Exchanges: Market Microstructure for Practitioners.* New York, NY: Oxford University Press.

Harrison, G. 2007. "Language as a Problem, a Right or a Resource?: A Study of How Bilingual Practitioners See Language Policy Being Enacted in Social Work." *Journal of Social Work* 7. https://doi.org/10.1177/1468017307075990

Hoadley, C. n.d. Chapter 12 "What is a Community of Practice and How Can We Support It?" in *Theoretical Foundations of Learning Environments*, ed. Land, S., and D. Jonassen, https://books.google.com/books?id=FJOoAgAAQBAJ&lr= (accessed May 2020).

Hornung, A., G. Krivosheev, N. Singh, and J. Bilger. 2006. "Standards Wars." Final Project, University of Washington, Seattle. https://courses.cs.washington.edu/courses/csep590a/06au/projects/standards-wars.pdf (accessed March 2020).

Houstoun, K., A. Milne, and P. Parboteeah. 2015. "Preliminary Report on Standards in Global Financial Markets." Report, May 11, Social Science Research Network https://doi.org/10.2139/ssrn.2531210 (accessed August 2019). https://bsigroup.com/en-US/Standards/Information-about-standards/What-is-a-standard/ (accessed January 4, 2021)

Hinskens, F., J.L. Kallen, and J. Taeldeman. n.d. "Merging and Drifting Apart. Convergence and Divergence of Dialects Across Political Borders."

International Journal of the Sociology of Language, no. 145 https://degruyter. com/view/j/ijsl.2000.issue-145/ijsl.2000.145.1/ijsl.2000.145.1.xml (accessed January 2020).

Hugoson, Mats-Åke. 2009. *"Centralized versus Decentralized Information systems: A HistoricalFlashback."* JönköpingInternationalBusinessSchool,Sweden,https:// link.springer.com/content/pdf/10.1007%2F978-3-642-03757-3_11.pdf (accessed March 2020).

Kettinger, W., and Y. Li. 2010. "The Infological Equation Extended: Towards Conceptual Clarity in the Relationship Between Data, Information and Knowledge." *Eur J Inf Syst* 19, 409–421. https://doi.org/10.1057/ejis.2010.25 (accessed February 2020).

Kuhl, K., and K. Barunmuller. n.d. "Stability and Divergence in Language Contact." https://books.google.com/books?id=CKtgBQAAQBAJ&printsec= frontcover#v=onepage&q&f=false (accessed February 2020).

Langefors, B. 1995. *Essays on Infology*, 159. Chartwell-Bratt.

Langefors, B. 1966. *Theoretical Analysis of Information Systems*, 197. Lund, Studentlitteratur.

Liberman, M. n.d. "Introduction to Linguistics." Syllabus. https://ling.upenn. edu/courses/Fall_2003/ling001/language_change.html (accessed April 2020).

Maginn, T., D.W. McLeavey, and J. Pinto. 2010. "Managing Investment Portfolios: A Dynamic Process." 3rd ed. New York, NY: Wiley.

McIntyre, H. 2007. *How the U.S. Securities Industry Works*, 3rd Edition. New York, NY: The Summit Group Publishing, Inc.

Merriam-Webster Online, https://merriam-webster.com/dictionary/lead (accessed August 2019).

Mincken, H.L. 1919. *The American Language*. Knopf.

Nichols, T.M. 2017. *The Death of Expertise*. New York, NY: Oxford University Press.

OMG. 2021. "Mission Statment." *Object Management Group*. https://omg.org/ about/index.htm (accessed January 4, 2021).

Organisation for Economic Co-operation and Development, Working Party #2 on Competition and Regulation. 2010. DAF/COMP/WP2/WD(2010)28. https://ftc.gov/sites/default/files/attachments/us-submissions-oecd-and-other-international-competition-fora/usstandardsetting.pdf (accessed August 2020).

OUCI-IOSCO. 2021. "CPMO IOSCO." *International Organization of Securities Commission.* https://iosco.org/about/?subsection=cpmi_iosco (accessed January 4, 2021).

Ritz, D. 2020. "Understanding Machine-Readability in Modern Data Policy." https://static1.squarespace.com/static/56534df0e4b0c2babdb6644d/t/5f1

b3496c6478514a73477bb/1595618455316/Understanding+Machine-Re adability+in+Modern+Data+Policy-7.24.2020-web.pdf. (accessed February 2020).

Ruíz, R. 1984. "Orientations in Language Planning." *NABE Journal* 8, 15–34. https://doi.org/10.1080/08855072.1984.10668464

Saba, W.S. 2018. "Language and its Commonsense: Where Logical Semantics Went Wrong, and Where it can (and should) go." Working Paper, May 22, semanticsarchive.net. (accessed August 2019).

Scott, S.V., and M. Zachariadis. 2013. *SWIFT: Cooperative Governance for Network Innovation, standards and community.* New York, NY: Routledge.

SEC Commissioner Gallagher, D.M. n.d. "Rules Applicable to U.S. Financial Services Holding Company Adopted Since July 2010." *Financial Services Holding Company Rules.* https://sec.gov/news/speech/2015/financial-services-holding-companies-rules-2.pdf (accessed January 4, 2021).

Smart Investor Staff. 2020. "10 Most Common Types of Bonds—Which Of Them Is Best For You?" *The Smart Investo*r. https://infoforinvestors.com/academy/bonds/types-of-bonds/ (accessed July 2020).

SMPG. N.d. "About us." *Securities Market Practice Group.* https://smpg.info/index.php?id=3 (accessed January 4, 2021).

Stanton, E.R. 1998. "Types of Bonds: 7 Bond Types Explained." *The Street.* https://thestreet.com/markets/rates-and-bonds/the-different-kinds-of-bonds-229831 (accessed June 2020).

SWIFT. n.d. "Payments Market Practice Group." https://swift.com/about-us/community/swift-advisory-groups/payments-market-practice-group (accessed January 4, 2021).

Tanenbaum, A. 1981. *Computer Networks,* New York, Pearson.

Tett, G. 2016. *The Silo Effect.* New York, Simon & Schuster.

The Giovannini Group. 2002. "Cross-Border Clearing and Settlement Arrangements in the European Union." *Economic Papers* 163, February, European Commission. URL: https://bit.ly/2J4opk5 (accessed August 2019).

The Investment Roadmap. n.d. http://iso20022.org/documents/general/InvestmentRoadmap.pdf (accessed August 2019).

The Investment Roadmap. n.d. https://isda.org/a/RciDE/press101210.pdf (accessed August 2019).

The Vinyl Institute. 2018. "Two-Faced Claims by the Iron Pipe Industry." https://vinylverified.com/blog/2018/8/29/two-faced-claims-by-the-iron-pipe-industry (accessed July 2020).

Trudgill, P. 1994. *Dialects.* Florence, KY: Ebooks Online Routledge.

Trudgill, P. 1994. *Dialects.* Routledge, Florence, KY, https://doi.org/10.4324/978 0203305935 (accessed August 2019).

U.S. Supreme Court. 1988. "Allied Tube v. Indian Head Inc., 486 U.S. 492." https://supreme.justia.com/cases/federal/us/486/492/ (accessed August 2020).

Wegner-Trayner. July 2020. "Introduction to Communities of Practice." https://wenger-trayner.com/introduction-to-communities-of-practice/

Wei, L. 2016. "New Chinglish and the Post-Multilingualism Challenge: Translanguaging ELF in China." *Journal of English as a Lingua Franca* 5, no. 1, 1–25 https://doi.org/10.1515/jelf-2016-0001 (accessed August 2019).

Wei, L. 2018. "Translanguaging as a Practical Theory of Language." *Applied Linguistics* 39, no. 2, https://doi.org/10.1093/applin/amx044 (accessed August 2019).

Weiss, D.M. 2006. *After the Trade is Made*. 3rd Revised edition. New York, NY: Portfolio.

World wide web consortium. 2021. "W3C Mission." https://w3.org/Consortium/mission (accessed January 4, 2021).

xBRL. 2021. "The Business Reporting Standard." https://xbrl.org/ (accessed January 4, 2021).

About the Author

Richard Charles Robinson is a senior executive with 30 years of experience in the financial industry, across operations and technology functions. He has worked throughout the front, mid, and back offices at major global custodian banks, brokerages, and industry utilities, leading transformative projects in data, operations workflow, and messaging.

For over 20 years, Rich, in addition to his full time jobs, has been heavily involved in the industry as an active participant of key working groups related to international data and messaging standards, including ISITC, FISD, EDM Council, ISO, ANSI/X9, ISDA, and SIFMA. He cofounded the first group on Unique Instrument Identification in 2000 and was a primary participant in the Best Practice work for ISO 15022. He was Convenor for the ISO Study Group on CFI's and UPI, and led the ISO Working Group on the Unique Transaction Identifier standard. Rich is on the Board of Directors of ISITC, serving as 2nd Vice Chair, and is lead Sherpa for the Asia Pacific Finance Forum's Financial Market Infrastructure Workstream on behalf of the Asian Business Advisory Council to the region's Finance Ministers.

A regular speaker at conferences, he has been published in the Journal of Securities Operations and Custody, Waters, and Inside Reference Data, among other global financial services publications. His 2018 paper, "A linguistics approach to solving financial services standardization," introduces the innovative idea of using applied linguistics to guide standards development and regulatory decisions, and was published in the Journal of Financial Markets Infrastructure. It was the original basis for this book.

Richard is currently Chief Strategist for Standards and Open Data at Bloomberg LLP. He works globally with regulators, legislators, and industry leaders on addressing data and standards issues to create more efficient and transparent markets. He holds an MBA in Organizational Behavior and Information Technology from NYU's Stern School and a BS in Industrial Management with a concentration in Management Information Systems from Carnegie Mellon University.

Rich, in his spare time, plays soccer (supports Fulham, NYRB, and the Riverhounds), surfs (yes, East Coast), snowboards, reads, gardens, plays guitar (poorly), and volunteers as a mentor for students and veterans entering the business world. He also writes some fiction (unpublished). He has three adult boys, Dylan, Kyle, and Gavin, of whom he is extremely proud, and they mean the world to him. His wife, Lisa, is an eighth grade History teacher, a constant source of inspiration, and love of his life. In addition to the boys, Lisa and Rich also care for a menagerie of three rescue dogs and a rescue cat.

Index

OTHER TITLES IN THE FINANCE AND FINANCIAL MANAGEMENT COLLECTION

John Doukas, Old Dominion University, Editor

- *Sustainable Finance and Impact Investing* by Alan S. Gutterman
- *The Non-Timing Trading System* by George O. Head
- *Small Business Finance and Valuation* by Rick Nason, and Dan Nordqvist
- *Finance for Non-Finance Executives* by Anurag Singal
- *Blockchain Hurricane* by Kate Baucherel
- *Risk Management for Nonprofit Organizations* by Rick Nason, and Omer Livvarcin
- *Understanding Behavioral BIA$* by Daniel C. Krawczyk, and George H. Baxter
- *Conservative Options Trading* by Michael C. Thomsett
- *Valuation of Indian Life Insurance Companies* by Prasanna Rajesh
- *Understanding Momentum in Investment Technical Analysis* by Micheal C. Thomsett
- *Understanding Cryptocurrencies* by Arvind Matharu
- *Mastering Options* by Philip Cooper
- *Trade Credit and Risk Management* by Lucia Gibilaro
- *Trade Credit and Financing Instruments* by Lucia Gibilaro
- *Escape from the Central Bank Trap, Second Edition* by Daniel Lacalle
- *The Art and Science of Financial Modeling* by Anrug Singal

Announcing the Business Expert Press Digital Library

Concise e-books business students need for classroom and research

This book can also be purchased in an e-book collection by your library as

- a one-time purchase,
- that is owned forever,
- allows for simultaneous readers,
- has no restrictions on printing, and
- can be downloaded as PDFs from within the library community.

Our digital library collections are a great solution to beat the rising cost of textbooks. E-books can be loaded into their course management systems or onto students' e-book readers. The **Business Expert Press** digital libraries are very affordable, with no obligation to buy in future years. For more information, please visit **www.businessexpertpress.com/librarians**. To set up a trial in the United States, please email **sales@businessexpertpress.com**.

www.ingramcontent.com/pod-product-compliance
Lightning Source LLC
Chambersburg PA
CBHW061208220326
41599CB00025B/4570

* 9 7 8 1 6 3 7 4 2 0 5 8 4 *